Table of Contents

Summary

Acknowledgments

About the presentations

Chapter 1. Anger in the Arab World and what the West can do

Chapter 2. Iraq: A desert mirage?

Chapter 3. Israel and Palestine; One state solution

Conclusion

Sources of data

The author

ISBN-13:
978-1541393233

ISBN-10:
1541393236

Summary

In 2004, I was asked to be an Advisor to the Coalition Provisional Authority (CPA) on private sector development in Iraq. As a result, I visited Iraq, where I grew up and still have a number of relatives and acquaintances, for the first time in 38 years.

Upon my return, I wrote a white paper which I sent to a few individuals at the CPA and Iraqi Governing Council. Its essence was twofold:

1. ***Build a private sector*** in Iraq to diversify the economy, create wealth, build a thriving middle class, and reduce the reliance on oil.
2. ***Decentralize all social activities*** to the 18 provinces. These included health, education, social services, religion, language, private sector, and most importantly public safety (police force).

This was an effort to build accountability and responsibility utilizing sound management principles including, measurable goals and outcomes, date-driven solutions, decentralization of decisions, and utilizing teams of stakeholders to develop "bottom-up" solutions. Unfortunately, these recommendations, which *were* consistent with the Federal Constitution of Iraq, went unheeded – with the exception of some segments of Iraqi Kurdistan.

Move forward ten years to 2014. The failure to implement the recommendations caused major problems: a budget shortfall estimated at $20 Billion, resulting from not diversifying and maintaining a large centralized government, and the invasion by Islamic State, which was enabled by resentment towards the central government for not decentralizing social activities especially the policing.

It is now evident, however, that some of the recommendations are being implemented - "bottom-up". For example, citizens in a few provinces, where insecurity was a problem, have finally begun to enforce law and order at the local level. Those Provinces have seen a decline in terrorist activities. It took longer than needed, but bottom-up has taken hold.

Elsewhere, the private sector has provided electricity through the use of small generators in neighborhoods to compensate the poor service provided by the central government. Recognizing this success, the central government has recently allowed private sector to invest in electricity generation on a larger scale.

Over the past 40 plus years, as an Engineer, Management Consultant, Entrepreneur and Advisor, the author has made hundreds of business presentations to clients covering the gamut of business and general management. Many of those presentations were related to solving strategic, operational and organizational issues, using facts and logic to help bottom-up teams develop sustainable solutions.

Over the past 12 years, this approach has been presented to address some of the intractable societal issues facing countries in The Middle East:

- *Anger in the Arab World*. The current approach to solving the problems in the Arab world is twofold; push them towards democracy and use force to fight the militant hard-liners. Managerially-proven, sustainable solutions require that the stakeholders develop their own solution in their own way
- *Iraq – a Desert Mirage?* The model practiced to-date is to help the Iraqis implement a centralized democracy along the western model. The workable solution is a highly decentralized representative government which relies on a functioning private sector middle class.
- *Israel and Palestine – a One State solution*. The current premise is to develop a two-state solution led by the international Community. The strategically pragmatic solution is for the two parties (Israelis and Palestinians) to create a single Federal Republic that is multi-cultural and pluralistic.

Acknowledgements

Without the effort of a very capable team, this two-part book would not have been created. I thank them all for making this a quality "bottom-up," effort.

Keith Rosenblum, a friend, journalist and past communications director for Congressman Jim Kolbe, (R-AZ, retired), helped me focus on the theme and title. He took dry, business-like style of writing and made it fun. He also interviewed colleagues to solicit perspectives of "bottom-up" management.

Barb Jardee, of Jardee Transcription, transcribed the audio from the presentation into notes that accompany each slide. Julia Denton edited the notes.

Kerry Trueman, of Anara Design, designed the covers.

The 20 plus individuals who reviewed the book draft and suggested changes.

Finally, the hundreds of individuals who attended the presentations, asked penetrating questions, challenged me and provided additional ideas and recommendations.

This book, in both parts, is dedicated to the individuals who attended the presentations over the past 12 years.

Chapter 22

My Testimony

First off, I would like to say to my lord in heaven, thank you for seeing me through, out of the darkness and into the light. I know that if it weren't for you, I could have never made it. Thank you so much for that!

Thank you for the love, joy, and happiness that you bring to me.

Thank you for the wisdom you give to me day after day to know right from wrong.

Thank you for giving me the willingness to give to others.

Thank you for the strength to carry on everyday, so that I can carry on for others.

Thank you for letting me be open to write this book and to share it with others.

Thank you for the tender heart that you have given to me.

Thank you for the tender conscience to do right by others.

Thank you for helping me be aware of my surroundings.

Thank you for helping my mom get through what she had to go through and being there for her, giving her strength when she needed it the most.

Thank you for putting my stepdad, Jim, in her life at the right time.

Thank you for helping her not to give up on me when I know at times she wanted to.

Thank you for giving my kids the wisdom and the strength to know that Mom would make it through.

Thank you for the most wonderful man that you have given to me, my husband Duane.

Thank you for the family I have now.

Thank you for my stepbrothers.

Thank you for my mentor, Angela.

I know that there is a reason for everything that we do in life. I know that God helped me write this book for a reason; the reason is so that I can help you. I also know that you have this book in your hands for a reason. I know that you can be whatever it is that you want to be, because God does not make junk, and you, my friend, are the best. I know that you can be the best in whatever it is that God wants you to be!

I hope that my story and what I went through gives you encouragement to *NEVER EVER GIVE UP ON YOURSELF.* I know that you will make it. Go for the *GOAL!* Pick yourself up, dust yourself off, and get back on the saddle. Today's your day. I feel it. You made the way. Believe it! I hope to meet you some day. *GOD WILLING!*

God bless and have a great day.

THE END

THANK YOU FOR LETTING ME SHARE!

About the presentations

The presentations in this book provide the bottom-up approach for dealing with three of the seminal issues facing the Middle East:

1. **Anger in the Arab World**. This chapter analyses the root causes of the anger in the Arab World and suggests appropriate strategic approaches the West may want to take to provide a long term sustainable solution.
2. **Iraq: A desert mirage?** Discusses the issues facing the country and the two possible outcomes based on the white paper developed in 2004 which utilized a highly decentralized operating model.
3. **Israel and Palestine; one state solution.** Discusses the difficulty of implementing a two-state solution and how a one-state solution can be beneficial to both inhabitants of this small land.

The presentations are the same offered different audiences over the past 12 years. Their purpose is to prompt audiences to ask questions and participate in developing practical solutions. They utilize data, analysis, proven template and structures, and logical arguments to suggest sound management solutions rather than those based on agendas or political viewpoints.

All past presentations were interactive. The body of a presentation typically consumes half the time, with the other half allocated to extensive Q&A. Audience input is garnered regularly and is utilized in subsequent versions of the presentation to strengthen the argument.

The presentations draw virtually all data from primary research sources -- organizations that conduct the research directly. These include, the Central Intelligence Agency (CIA) World Factbook, Organization for Economic Co-operation and Development (OECD) United Nations and its entities, The World Bank, Fund for Peace, and Transparency International, among others. Books and special studies are utilized for medieval or prehistoric data and forecasts. A list of the data sources and books reviewed are included under Sources of Data.

This book was written in a format of "text-plus-presentations," with notes elaborating each slide. Please review the presentations in sequence as the information in one presentation is relevant to a subsequent presentation.

Such has been the enthusiastic endorsement by the host groups that it has served as a catalyst for this initiative. See sample comments on the next page:

"Saad Allawi's presentation on "Anger in the Arab World" provided both historical and contemporary understanding of the current mindset of the Middle East. His talk was comprehensive and easily understood for such a complex subject. The questions from the audience in the subsequent Q and A session showed how he piqued interest and a desire for more information on the part of the attendees". *Carol Tierney, Forum Team, Casas Adobes Congregational Church UCC*

"I have had the good fortune to hear Saad Allawi make two separate presentations on the Middle-East, *Anger in the Arab World* and *Iraq: A Desert Mirage?* His perspective on the situation in the Arab world is unique, very informative and obviously well researched. I learned so much more from his presentations than from any news outlet". *Liz Curtis Cohn, 2015-2018 Rotary District 5500 District Administrator*

"For those who want greater insight and knowledgeable first hand commentary of the Arab world, Saad Allawi delivers in a remarkable way. The data he shares and the history and culture associated with the Arab people are important to understand if we are to see the world through their eyes. This becomes important if we are to try and solve the problems that we face in our interactions with them as a people. Even those who disagree with Saad's conclusions are enlightened and better equipped to judge for themselves the issues we face today." *Jeff Utsch, Heirs of The Republic*

Excellent summary of the history and conflicts in the Middle East. Mr. Allawi shows us precisely why the Arab countries are so complex to understand and how the West has historically misunderstood the nature of the conflict in that region". *A. Agarwal, Adjunct Professor - International Business, Eller College of Management*

"Saad Allawi exudes great confidence in his presentations and in his data. He never fails to stimulate discussion." *Philip J. Silvers, PhD, Past Director, Rotary International*

The presentations are proprietary and cannot be used for copying, distribution or presentations. If you would like to do so, contact the author for permission and alternatives at sjallawi@gmail.com.

Chapter 1
Anger in The Arab World

The current approach to solving the problems in the Arab world is twofold; push society toward democracy, and use force to fight the militant hard-liners. Managerially proven solutions mean that the stakeholders develop their own resolutions in their own way.

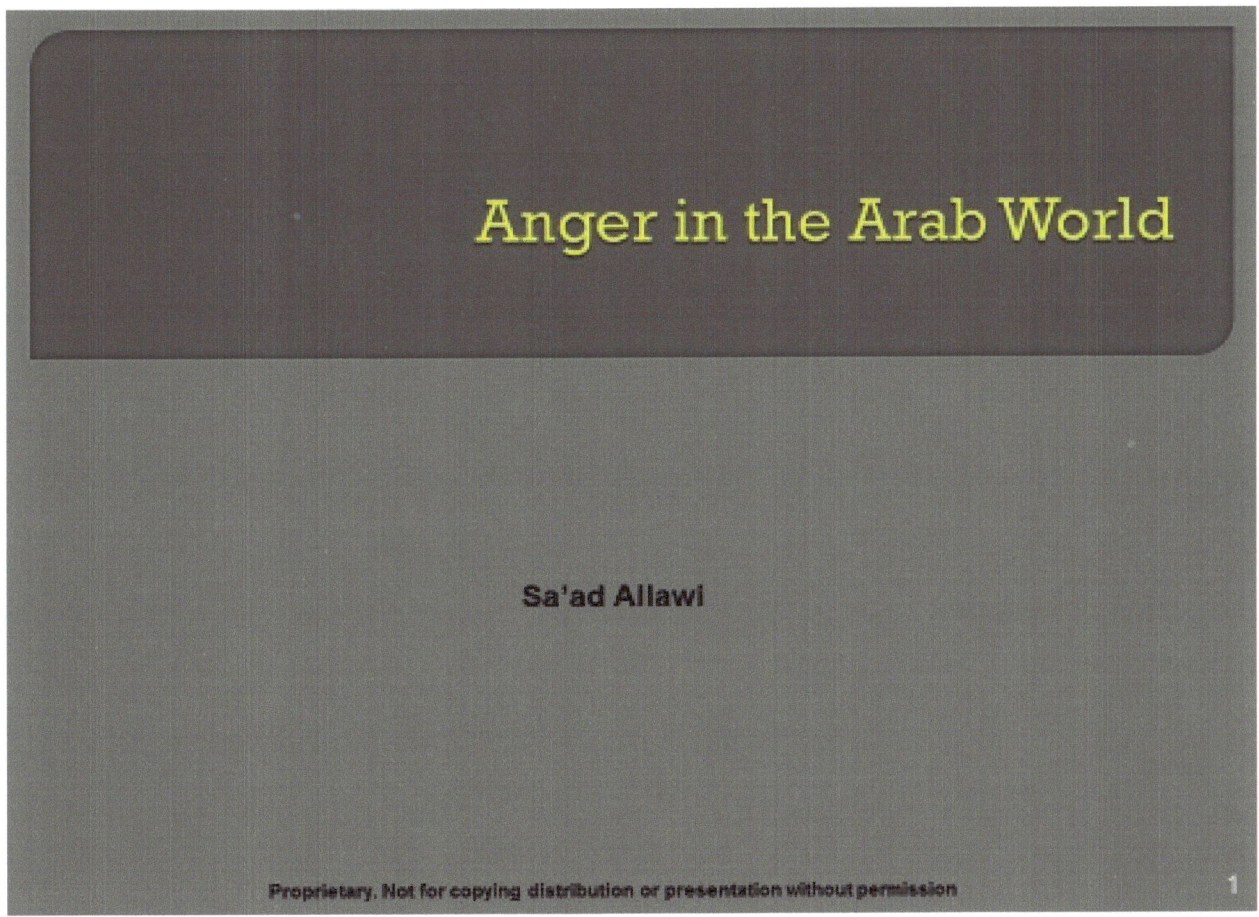

This presentation reviews briefly the history and demographics of the Arab World in the context of the larger Muslim world. It discusses the root causes of the anger generated in recent history (gross inequality, endemic corruption, poor performance, very little freedom, failure of Modernism, injustice from the West, and a bleak future). It discusses the demographics of the countries in the Middle East and how they were cobbled together by the British and French after WWI. It talks about the Middle East Project and how to re-draw the map based on ethnic and sectarian lines.

The presentation will cover the following: the modern history of the Arab world, root causes of anger, current manifestations, and the suggested response by the West.

© Grassroots Metamorphosis Part 2. Sa'ad J Allawi. Proprietary

Muslim world

I. Modern History – Moslem World

- 1.5 to 1.9 Billion – 23% of the world

- Most are non-Arabs – 80%

- Two main branches – Sunnis (85%) and Shiites (15%)

- Modern and conservatives – e.g. Indonesia, KSA

- Ultra-conservative – Salafists and Wahhabis (Est. at 4%)

3

There are an estimated 1.5 to 1.9 billion Muslims in the world, representing 23% of the world's population. Muslims are present in every continent; sixty-two percent of Muslims live in the Asia Pacific Region, and the remaining Muslims live in the Middle East, North Africa, Sub-Saharan Africa, Europe, and the Americas. Most Muslims (80%) are not Arabs and hail from countries such as Turkey, Iran, and Afghanistan, Indonesia, Pakistan, India, Malaysia, Nigeria, Ethiopia, Albania, and Bulgaria. There are two main branches in Islam: Sunni (85%) and Shiites (15%).

Muslim countries can be placed into two categories (my own definition) – modern and conservative. Countries practicing modern Islam (e.g. Turkey and Indonesia) successfully amalgamated secularism and modernity with Islamic law. Conservative countries (e.g. Saudi Arabia and Iran) rely much more heavily on Islamic law for governance. Then there are the ultra-conservatives, the Salafists and the Wahhabis, who abide by eighteenth-century doctrine. Salafists and Wahhabis represent approximately 4% of the total Sunni population, and within that group, there are an estimated 100 thousand to 200 thousand fighters who belong to the Al-Qaeda, Islamic State, and their affiliates.

Greater Middle East

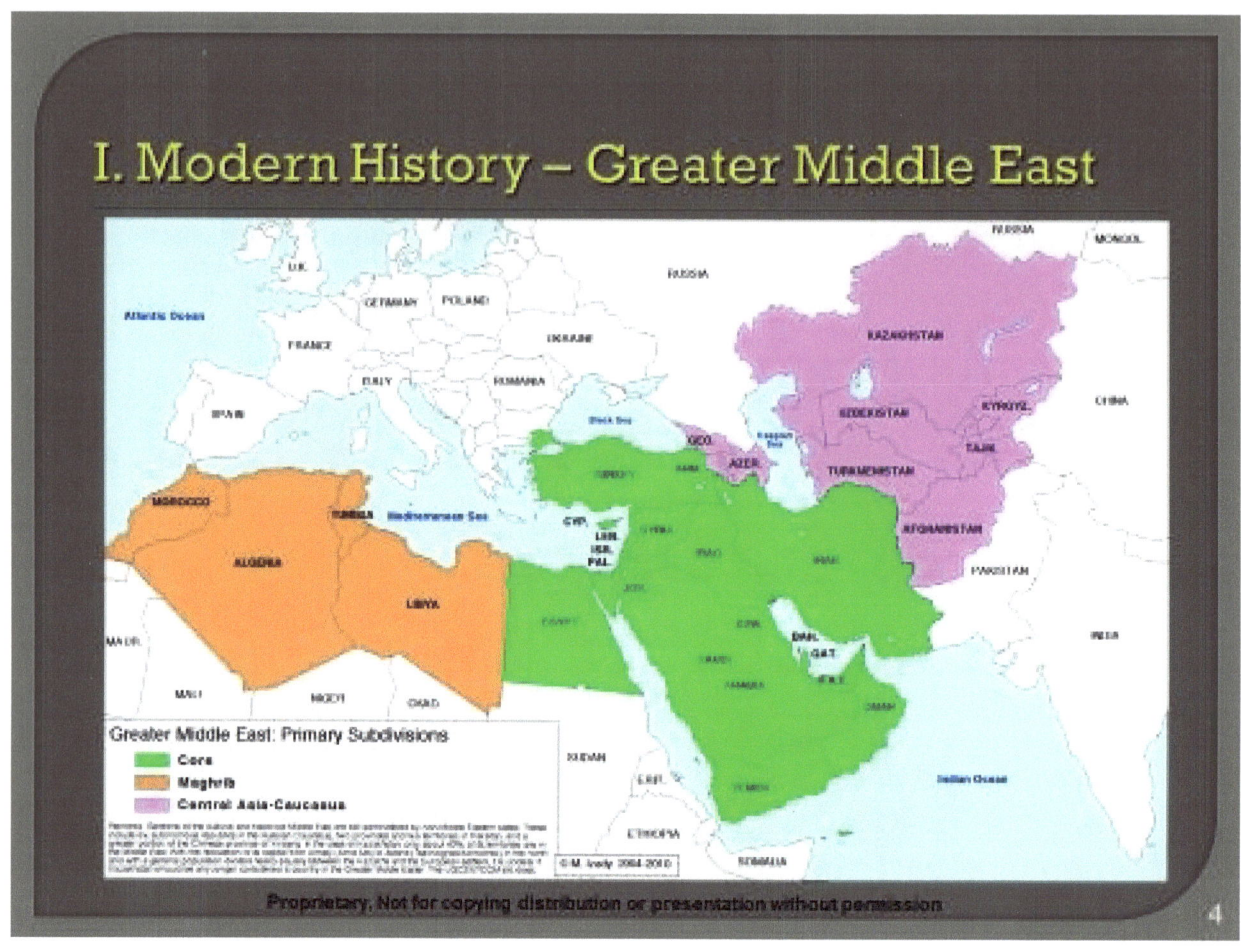

Starting with the map of the greater Middle East, the green part in the middle is the core Middle East, the orange part on the left-hand side (western) is the Maghreb or North Africa, and the purple part on the right-hand side is Central Asia and the Caucuses.

This presentation will deal primarily with the Arab world, which encompasses North Africa and countries in the core Middle East, with the exception of Turkey and Iran, which are not Arab countries.

What is the Arab world?

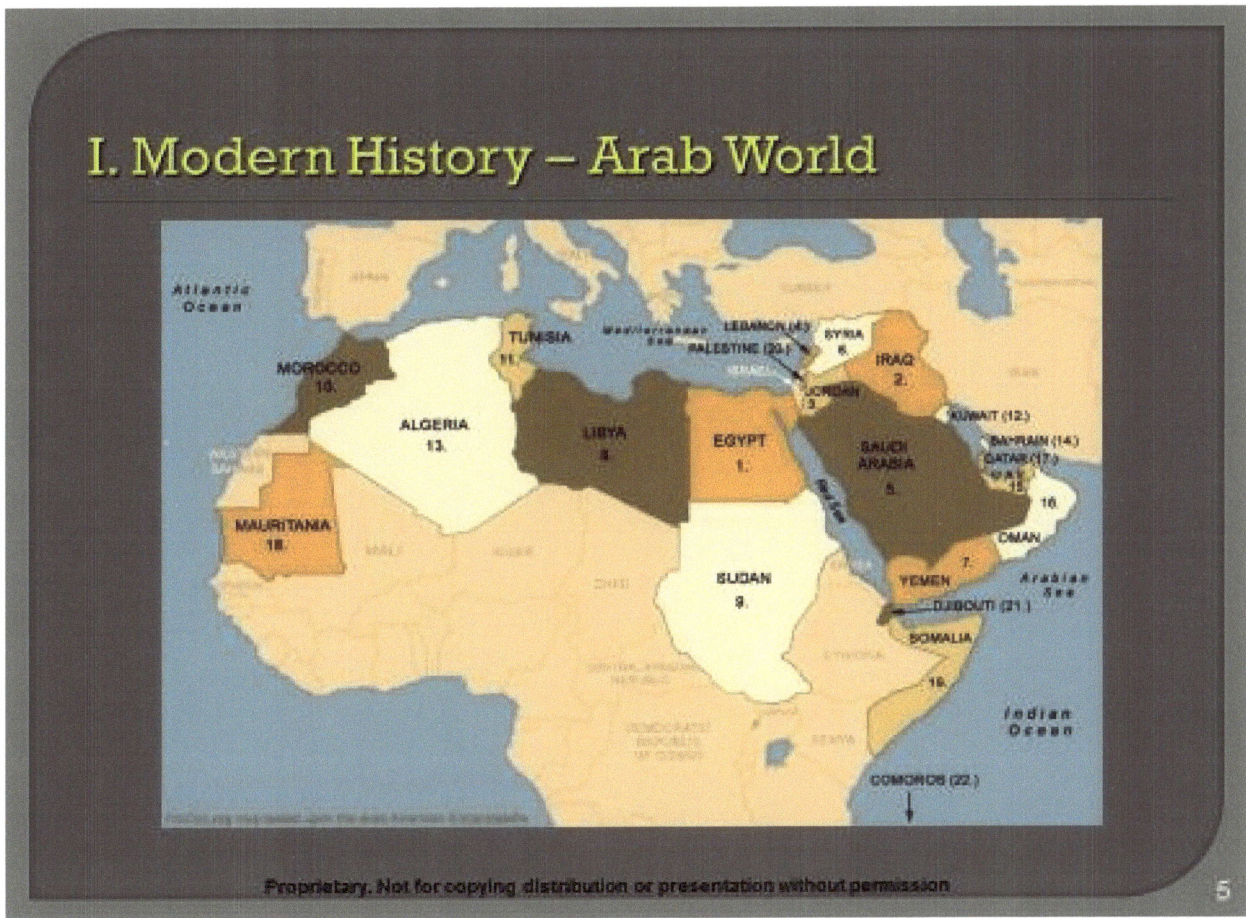

The Arab world includes twenty-two countries that are members of the Arab League. Most of these countries utilize Arabic as the official state language. The Arab countries start in the west (left-hand side of the map) with Mauritania, and end with Oman to the east. This presentation discusses the issues facing the Arab world.

Milestones

In the 1920s, Egypt became independent as a country. In the 1930s, Iraq, Saudi Arabia followed. In the 1940s, Jordan, Syria, and Lebanon then became independent. In the 1950s, Libya, Tunisia, Morocco, and Sudan also gained independence. In the 1960s, Mauritania, Kuwait, Algeria, Yemen, and Somalia did so. In the 1970s, Oman, Bahrain, United Arab Emirates, Qatar, and Djibouti gained independence. **Conclusion: these are new countries. With a few exceptions, most have not had their independence for much longer than sixty years.**

In terms of democracy and free elections, Lebanon is the oldest. It started with free elections in the early 1950s and continued since that time, with a hiatus during its civil war (1975 to 1990). Yemen had its first free election in 1990 when the two Yemeni countries (North and South) were combined, and then again later in 2011. Iraq had its first free election in 2004 and has held three subsequent to that.

Tunisia, Egypt, and Libya had elections in 2011 and 2012, after the Arab Spring (The large scale demonstrations that took place in many countries of the Arab word demanding reform or change of government)

While these countries are new, they are even newer democracies, and most of them have not had any free elections or representative government for more than ten years.

I. Modern History - Evolution

- 1920 to 1940 – Uncertainty
- 1940 to 1960 – Yearning for independence
- 1960 to 1980 – Polarization and new political ideologies
- 1980 to 2000 – Ethnic and religious divisions
- 2000 to Date – US led intervention

Proprietary. Not for copying distribution or presentation without permission

7

1920 to 1940 was a period of uncertainty, with strong Western colonial influence and transition into the modern world. Between 1940 and 1960, there was yearning for independence and resistance to colonization. Israel was created in 1948. There were revolutions in Egypt, Iraq, Syria, and Algeria and the Suez Canal War in 1956.

From 1960 to 1980, the area witnessed polarization and new political ideologies. There was the Western camp and the Soviet Union camp—some countries belonged in the Western camp, such as Jordan, the Gulf States, and Morocco. Others belonged in the Soviet Union camp, such as Iraq, Syria, Egypt, Algeria, and Libya. This period saw the growth of Arab Nationalism, Communism, and Ba'athism and two wars with Israel (in 1967 and 1973).

The period of 1980 to 2000 witnessed ethnic and religion divisions. These included the civil wars in Lebanon, Algeria, and Sudan; the Iran-Iraq War; and the first Gulf War.

During the years from 2000 to date, U.S.-led intervention occurred. The U.S. took leadership in the Middle East from the French and the British. The second Gulf War and the Arab Spring took place.

Now let us talk about U.S. support.

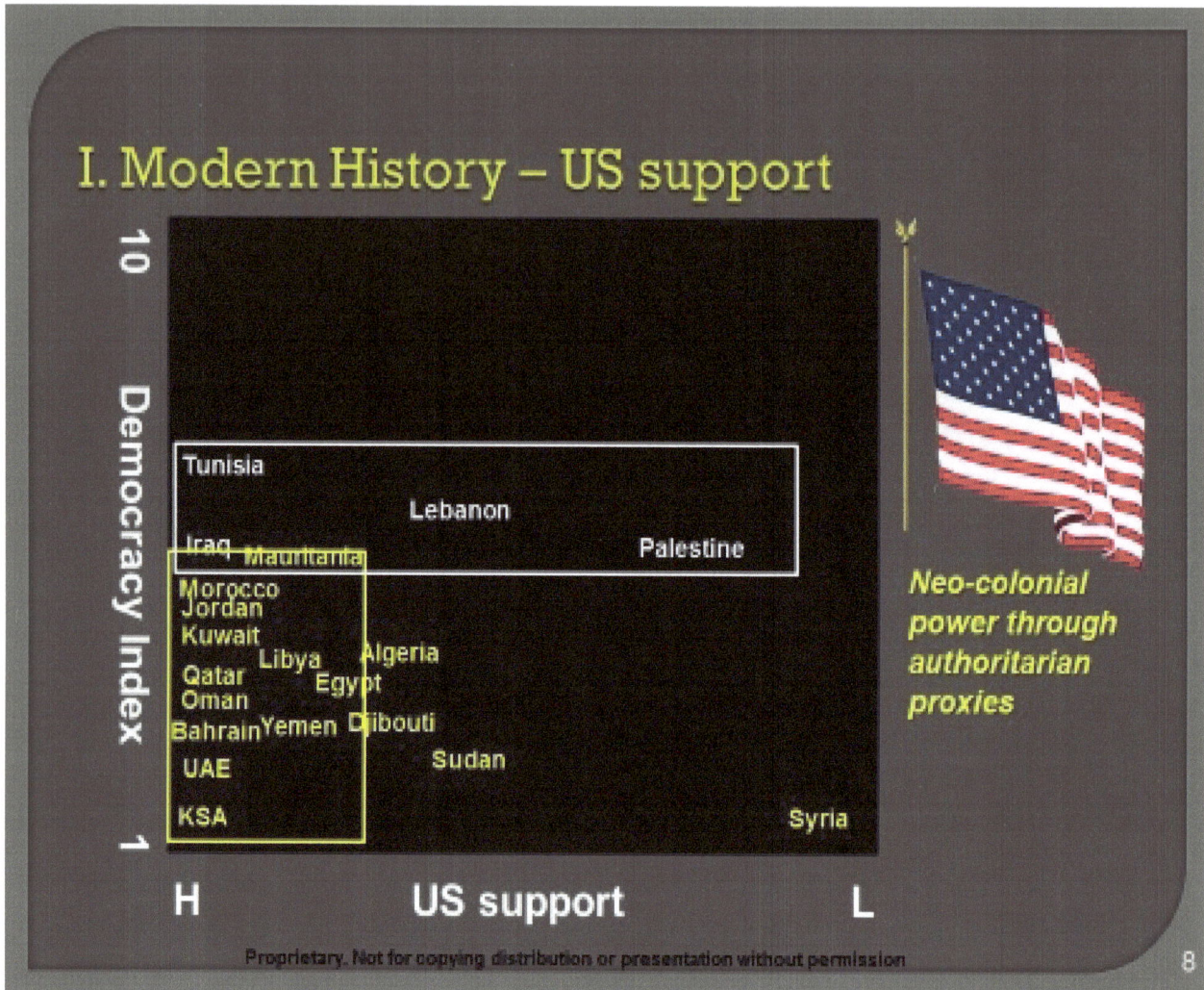

On this matrix, the "Y" axis is the democracy index from 1 to 10 (ten being the most democratic or most representative government). The "X" axis is the U.S. support to those countries (from high to low). Observe the Arab countries on that grid, the ones in yellow are less democratic, and the ones in white are a little bit more democratic. Look at where the U.S. support (yellow box) is strongest; it lines up with many of the less-democratic regimes.

Among the countries that are a little bit more democratic, there is strong U.S. support for Iraq and Tunisia, and less so for Lebanon and Palestine. While the U.S. doesn't have military forces on the ground (except for Iraq and, to a lesser extent, Syria), the U.S. exercises its influence through authoritarian regimes.

Because of this, most people in the Arab world view the U.S. as a new colonial power. This exercise of power by proxy doesn't apply just to the U.S.; it also applies to the Western European countries that have supported those authoritarian countries in the Arab World.

Arab spring

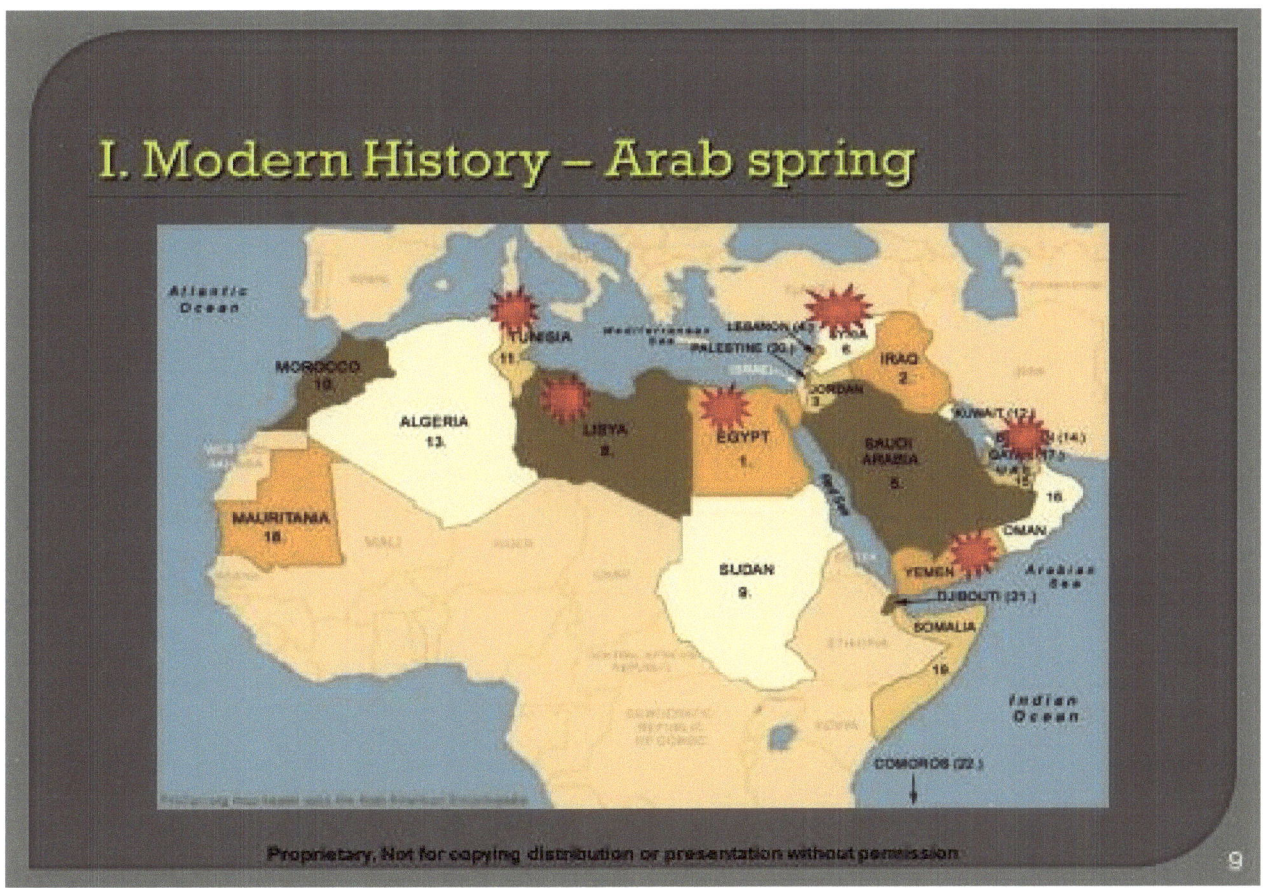

In 2011, the Arab Spring started in Tunisia, followed by Libya, Egypt, Syria, Bahrain, and Yemen. In some of these countries, the Arab Spring has degenerated into civil or turf war (in Syria, Yemen, and Libya). During this year, Egypt saw a change of government by the military. Tunisia has been the most stable country since the Arab Spring.

Let us go over the root causes of the unrest in the Arab World.

The first is gross inequality among and within Arabic countries.

II. Root cause of the unrest – Gross Inequality (low is more equal)

Among the countries in the region (GDP/Capita)
- Average for the Arab Countries - $16,501
- Qatar - $143,400 (world highest)
- Somalia $600
- US – $54,600

Within each country (GINI score)
- Average for Arab Countries – 37 (understated)
- Iraq – 30
- Qatar – 41
- Sweden – 25
- US - 41

Proprietary. Not for copying distribution or presentation without permission

10

The average Gross Domestic Product per-capita for the Arab countries is $16,500. The range is very broad. Qatar has a per-capita income of $143,000. It is the highest in the Arab world and the highest in the world as a whole. Somalia, at the other extreme, has a per-capita income of $600. By comparison, the U.S. per-capita Gross Domestic Product is $54,600.

Inequality within the countries utilizing the World Bank's GINI score*, the average for the Arab countries is 43, which shows a level of inequality. This is an understated statistic, because most of the Gulf states with high inequality do not report. The score for Iraq is 30. Qatar's score is 41. By contrast, Sweden has a score of 25, which indicates a higher level of equality. By comparison, the score for the U.S. is 41.

*The GINI score ranges from 1 to 100. The higher the score, the lower the equality of a country, and the lower the score, the more equality.

The next cause of unrest is endemic corruption.

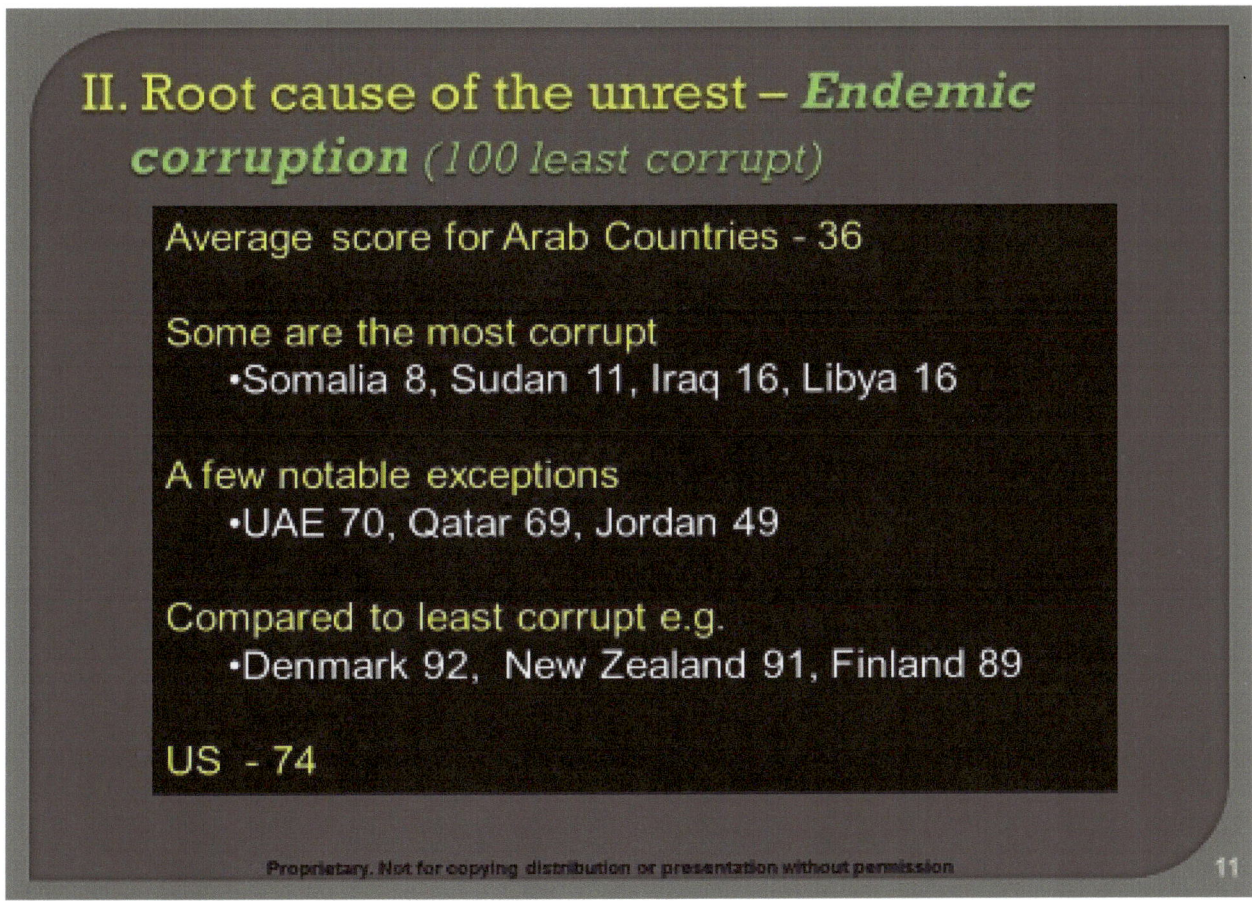

The scores used to measure each country range from 1 to 100, where 100 represents low corruption and 1 represents high corruption.

The average score for the Arab countries is 36, which indicates a high level of corruption.

Some countries are very corrupt, including Somalia (8), Sudan (11), Iraq (16), and Libya (16). A few countries in the region demonstrate low corruption, including the United Arab Emirates (70), Qatar (69), and Jordan (49). Compare those scores to those of the least corrupt countries around the world: Denmark (92), New Zealand (91), and Finland (89). By comparison, the U.S. scores at 74.

The next cause of unrest is poor performance.

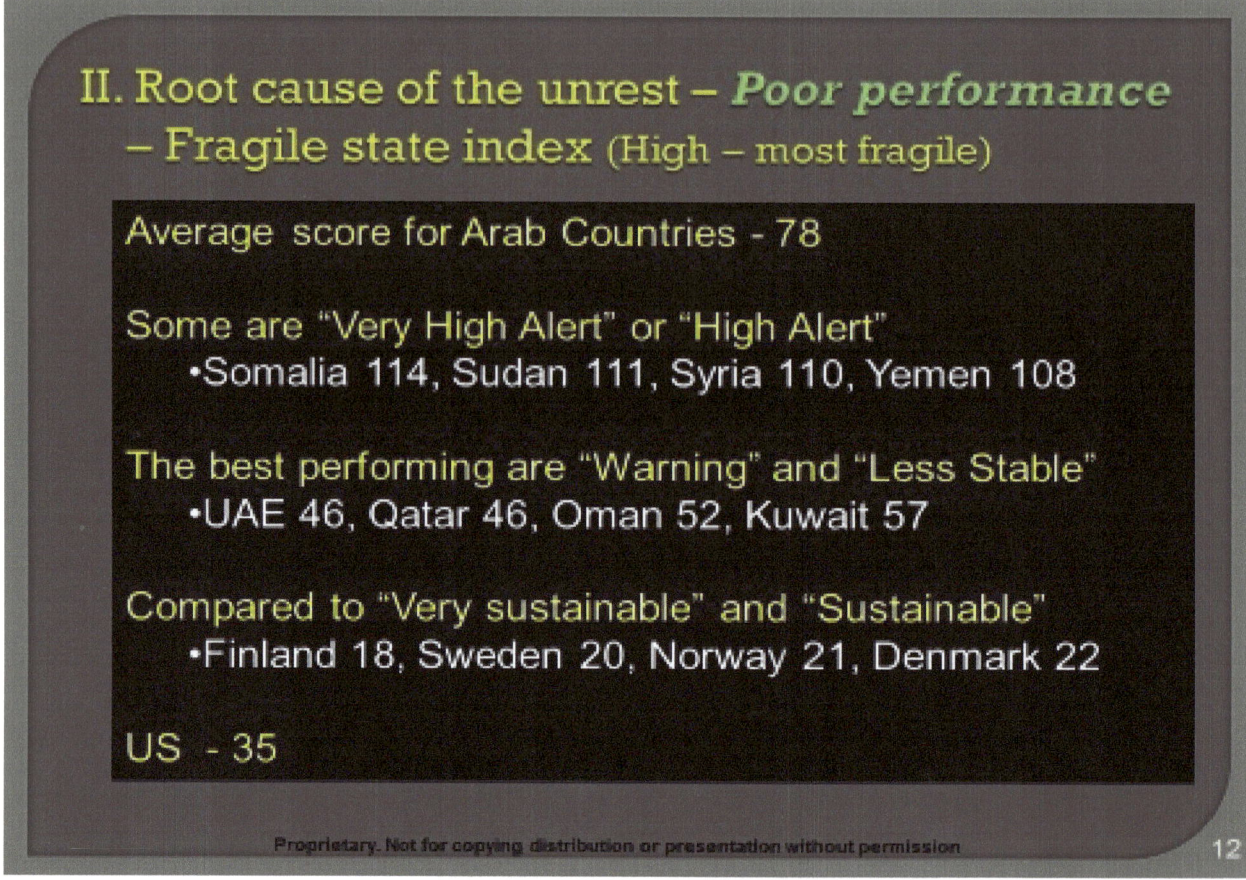

Here, the Fragile States Index* is used to compare the Arab countries, and the higher the score, the more fragile the country is. There are six ranges of fragility; very sustainable to very high alert. Very high alert means risk of failure as a country. A very sustainable country can sustain itself.

The average score for the Arab World is 78, which indicates high alert.

Some Arab countries are at very high alert or high alert, such as Somalia (114), Sudan (111), Syria (110), and Yemen (108). The best-performing countries within the Arab world are still in the Warning and Less Stable category. Those are the United Arab Emirates (46), Qatar (46), Oman (52), and Kuwait (57).

Compare the Arab countries to others in the Very Sustainable and Sustainable categories, such as Finland (18), Sweden (20), Norway (21), and Denmark (22).

By comparison, the U.S. scores 35 in this category.

*Fragile States Index is a score that identifies how stable a country is based on a number of political, economic, financial, and demographic criteria. The higher the score, the lower the stability.

To assess the Arab countries' performance in a different way, they are compared to Spain.

II. Root cause of the unrest – *Poor performance* - e.g. compared to Spain

Measure	Arab Countries	Spain	Variance
Population	368.2	48.2	
GDP	$6,076	$1,570	
Per Capita GDP	$16,501	$33,700	104%
Life expectancy	70.5	83.0	18%
Infant mortality	30.3	3.3	89%
Percent literacy	78.7	98.1	25%
Life expectancy for school	10	15	50%
Number of Universities	590	1415	140%
Nobel Prize winners	6	7	17%
Freedom of the press	42	23	45%

13

The comparison with Spain was conducted for two reasons: first, it's a medium-sized country, and as such these countries were not compared to economic powerhouses like the U.S., Japan, and China. Secondly, Spain was under Arab occupation for 500 years.

This comparison confirms that Arab countries compare unfavorably to Spain:

- Spain has a higher Gross Domestic Product per-capita by 104%
- Life expectancy is 18% longer in Spain
- Infant mortality in Spain is 89% lower
- Literacy is 25% higher for the Spanish
- Duration of education is 50% longer
- Number of universities in Spain is 140% greater
- There are 17% more Nobel Prize winners in Spain
- Freedom of the press is 45% higher in Spain

Keep in mind that Spain has a population of 48 million, whereas the Arab countries have a combined population of 368 million.

The next root cause of anger is the lack of freedom.

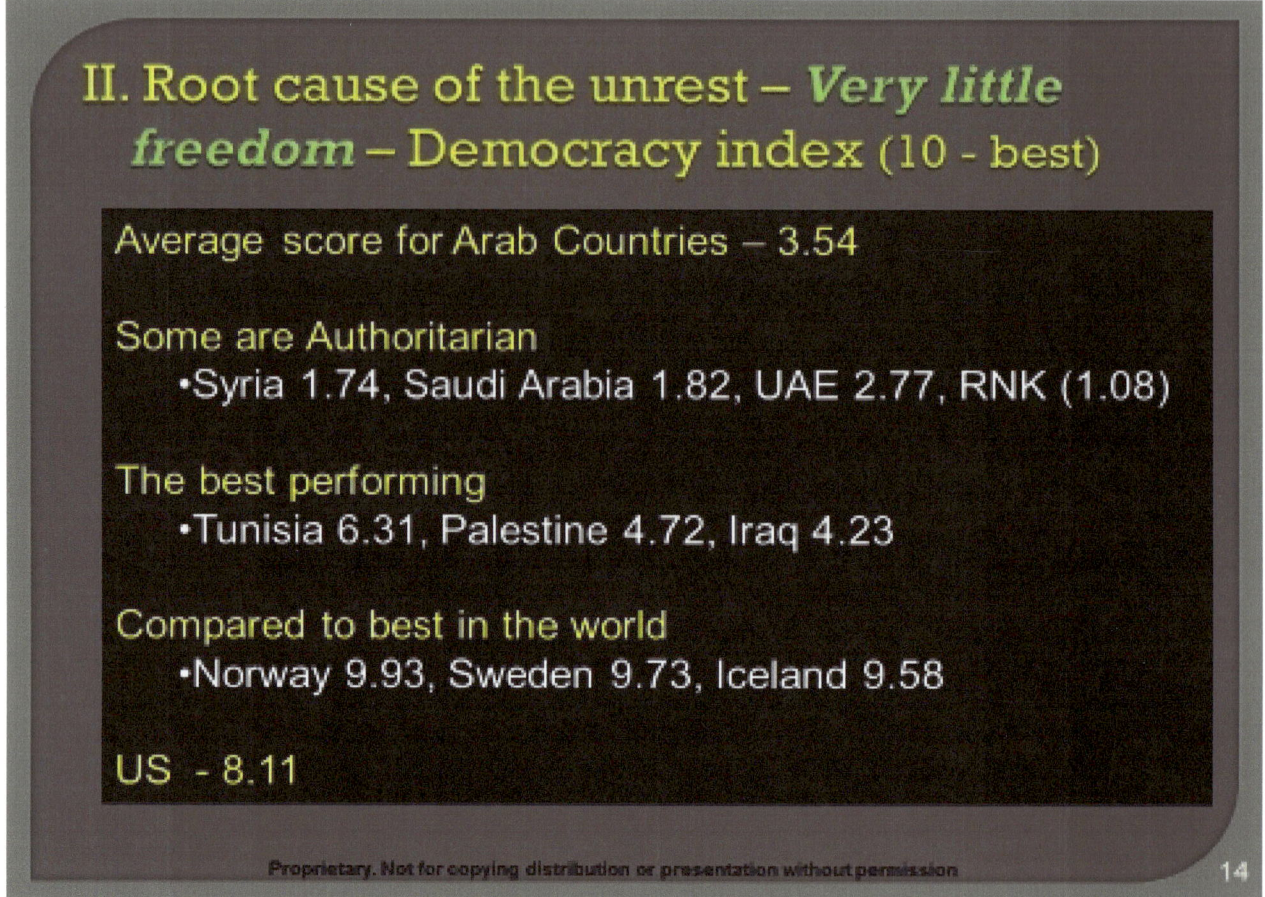

To measure this, the democracy index (shown in an earlier slide) was utilized. A score of 10 indicates the most democracy, and 1 indicates the least.

The average for Arab countries on the democracy index is 3.54, which is low.

Some countries are outright authoritarian, such as Syria (1.74), Saudi Arabia (1.82), and the United Arab Emirates (2.77). North Korea, one of the least free countries in the world, has a score of 1.08. The best performing countries in the Arab world are Tunisia at 6.31, Palestine at 4.72, and Iraq at 4.23.

We compare the Arab countries to the most democratic nations in the world, including Norway with a score of 9.93, Sweden at 9.73, and Iceland at 9.58. By comparison, the U.S. score is 8.11.

The next cause of unrest is failure of modernism.

A number of Arab countries tried Western secularism, which failed. South Yemen, before it merged with North Yemen, instituted Marxism, which failed. Some Arab countries, including Algeria, Libya, Egypt, and Iraq, tried socialism, which also failed. In the 1950s and 1960s, a number of Arab countries tried nationalism. That also failed.

The next cause of unrest is injustice by the West.

Western support of autocrats could be economic, financial, political, diplomatic, or military in nature. Economic or financial support often ends up in the pockets of the autocrats running the country, not the 90% plus who are being ruled, which creates resentment.

Double standards are frequently applied by the West. For example, in Syria, the West has pressured the Assad government heavily

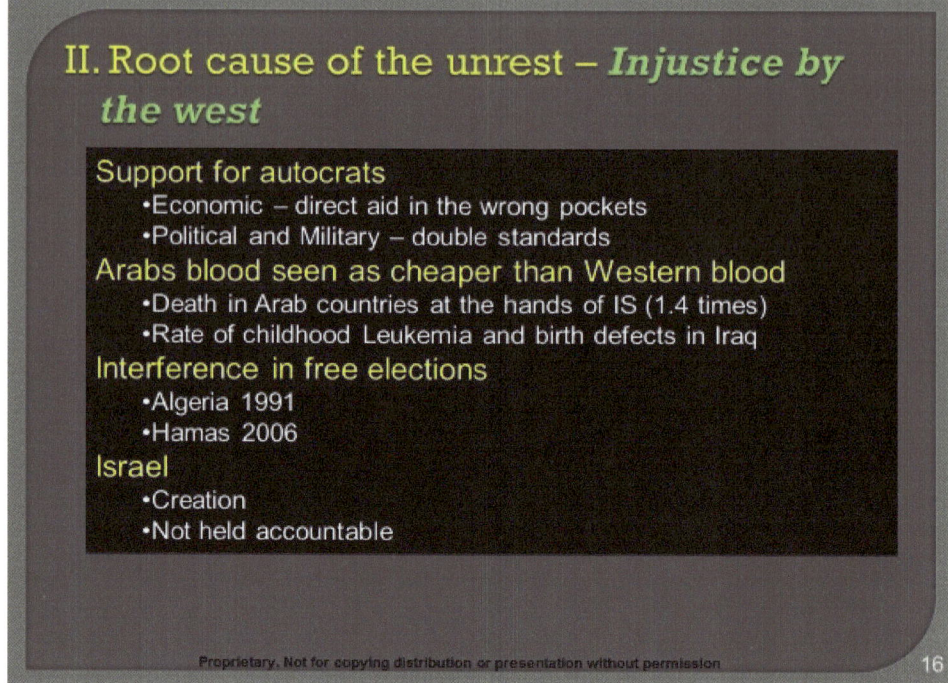

because of their action against their own population. Yet when it came to Bahrain, an ally of the west, there was virtually no pressure when the government of that country used force to suppress the Arab spring.

Arab blood is seen as cheaper than Western blood. For example, Western press coverage of deaths that occurred at the hands of Islamic State and their sympathizers in non-Arab countries is extensive. Yet, when many deaths occur in the Arab countries at the hands of Islamic State during similar periods, there is very little mention, if at all.

The rate of childhood leukemia and birth defects in Iraq is significantly higher (6 times the world rate of leukemia and 80% birth defects in places such as Fallujah). Many of the International Health organizations that have experienced this phenomenon believe it is likely to be caused by the allies' use of depleted uranium in ammunitions in the first and second Gulf Wars. However, there is hardly a debate on that issue and the World Health Organization has refused to release its data on this issue.

Arab nations saw Western interference in free elections. Algeria had a free election in 1991 in which the Islamists won. The West didn't like it and encouraged a successful military takeover. A serious insurgency, bordering on civil war, took place, during which 200,000 people died. In 2006, Hamas won a free election in Palestine by a landslide. The West was surprised and shocked, and because Hamas was declared a terrorist organization, the West forced the leadership of the Palestinian Authority to go to Fatah, which polled in a distant third.

Israel received special treatment. Nobody took into consideration the opposition of more than 90% of the people living in that part of the world for the creation of Israel in 1948. Israel is also seen to be above international law, having not abided by over 50 United Nations resolutions without facing consequences.

The frustration in the Arab world will only increase.

II. Root cause of the unrest – Frustration will only increase

Percent of global GDP declining
- 5% currently
- 3% by 2050

Youth Unemployment
- 30% in 2015 – worst region in the world
- 16% for Developed Economies
- 10% for South Asia

Water shortages – Worst region in the World

17

In 2010, the contribution of Middle East and North Africa to the World's Gross Domestic Product was 5%. It is projected to drop to 3% by 2050, with an equal drop in influence.

In 2015, youth unemployment in the Arab world was the highest globally at 30%. By comparison, the developed economies have 16% youth unemployment, and in South Asia this figure is 10%.

The Middle East and North Africa are also the worst regions in the world for water shortages.

In summary

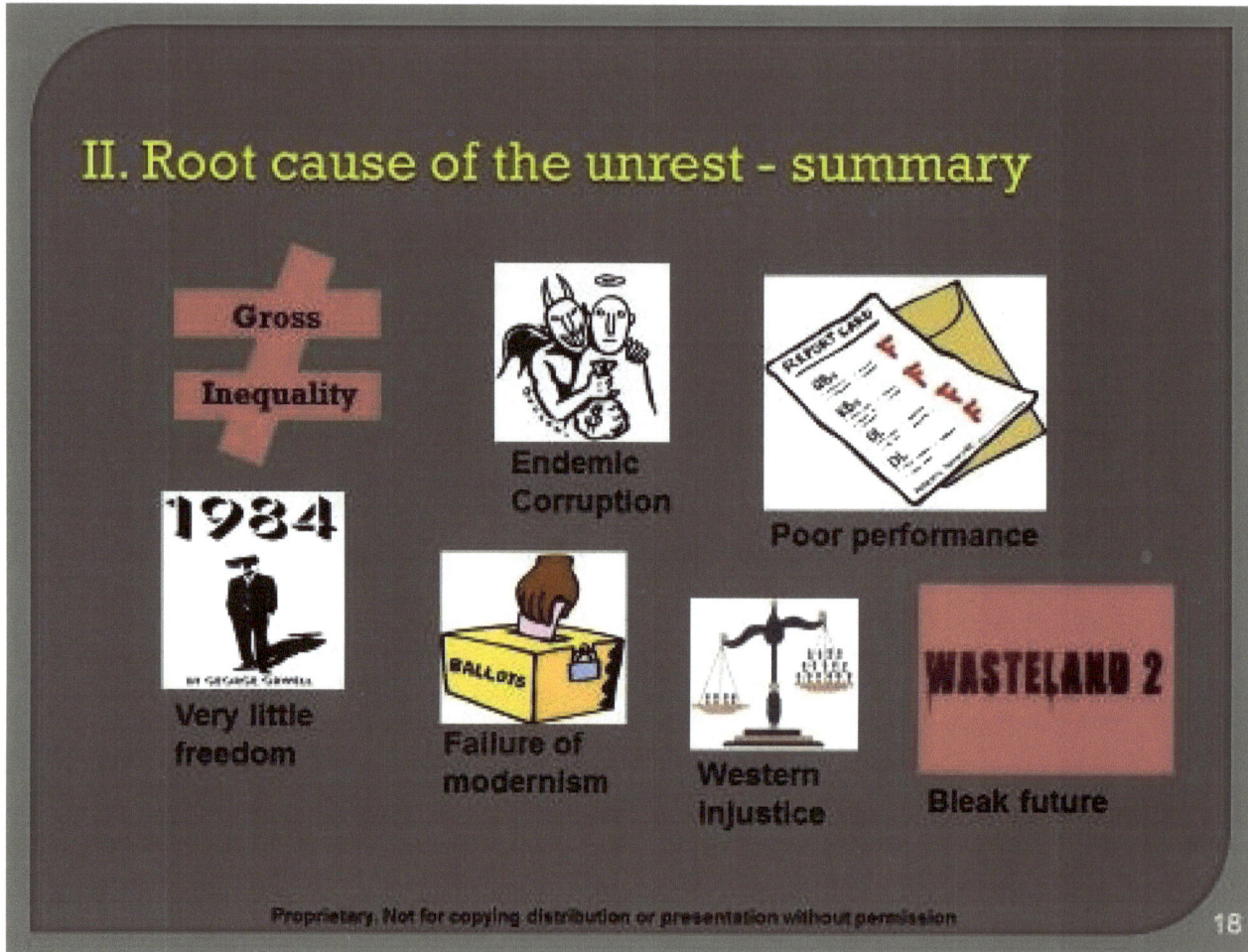

The root causes of unrest in the Arab World are gross inequality, endemic corruption, poor performance, very little freedom, failure of modernism, Western injustice, and a bleak future.

These are the reasons most people in the Arab World are frustrated and angry and can you blame them.

Many people in the Arab world look back with great yearning at a time when the Arab world was the world's superpower (800 to 1258 A.D.) and lament their current state. Centuries ago, Arabs were great contributors to and leaders in arts, literature, philosophy, science, medicine, and technology. Their footprint extended west of Spain all the way to the borders of China.

What happened to many of those countries that had free elections as a result of the Arab Spring in 2011-2012?

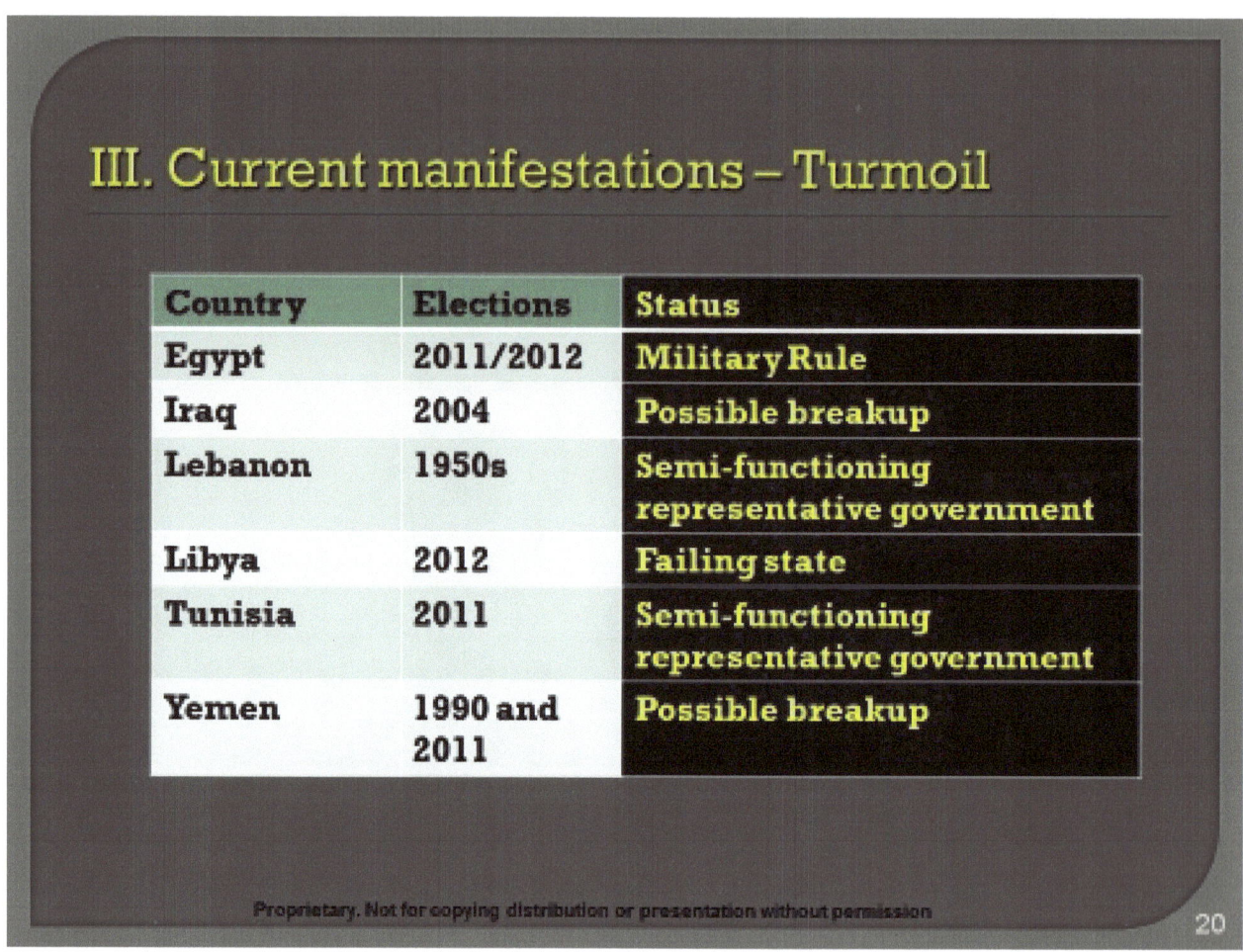

Great turmoil is the best way to describe the current state. Egypt is under military rule. Iraq could possibly divide. Lebanon has a semi-functioning representative government. Libya is a failing state. Tunisia is a semi-functioning representative government and the one that's most likely to survive. Yemen is also likely to divide.

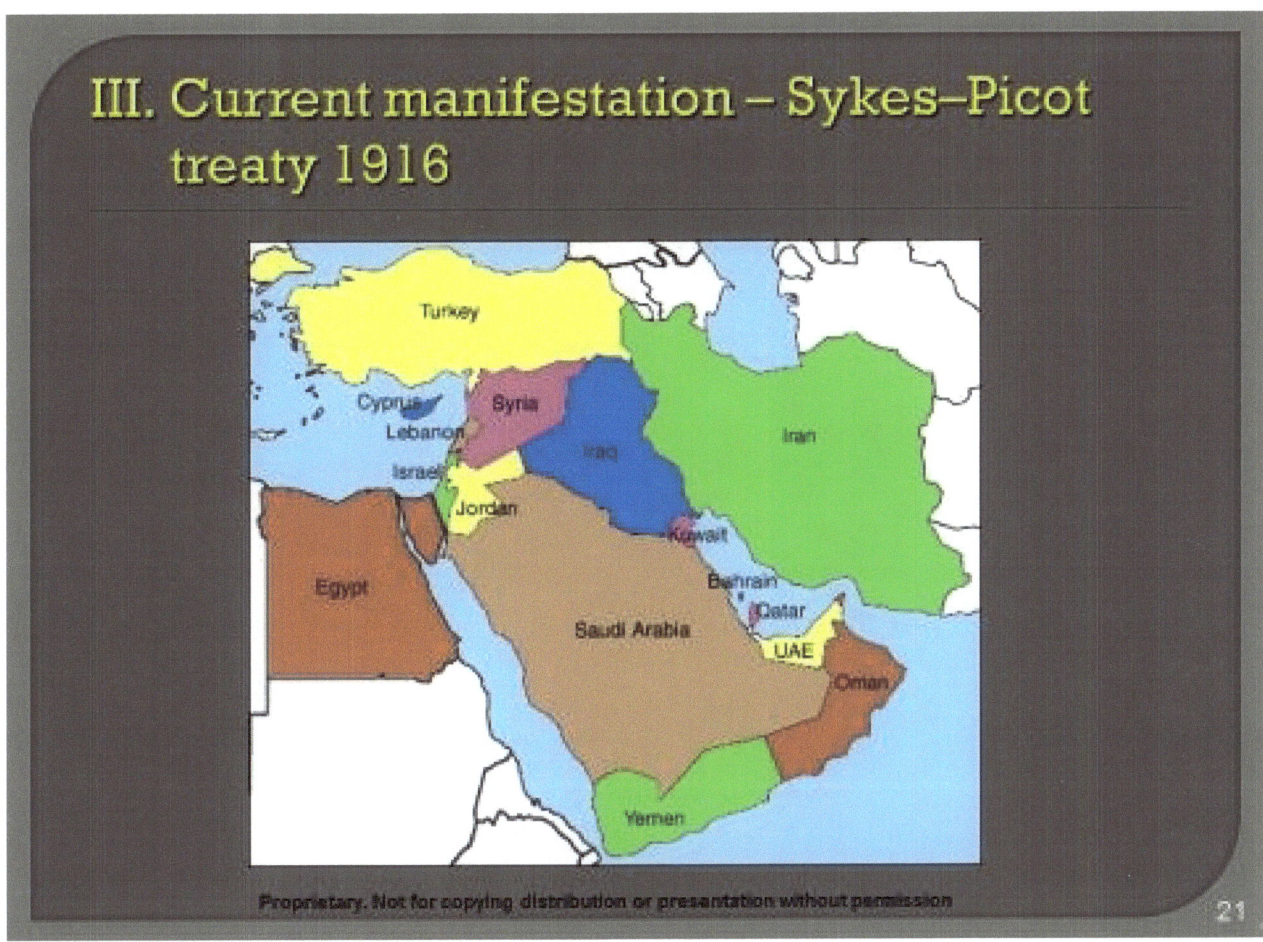

In 1916, a treaty was reached called Sykes-Picot. It was a British-French treaty to divide the Ottoman Empire after the World War I into the countries of the Middle East.

This map shows the divisions as outlined by this treaty. However, not much thought was given to people of the same sect, religion, and ethnic backgrounds in dividing up those countries, causing many of today's problems in the Middle East.

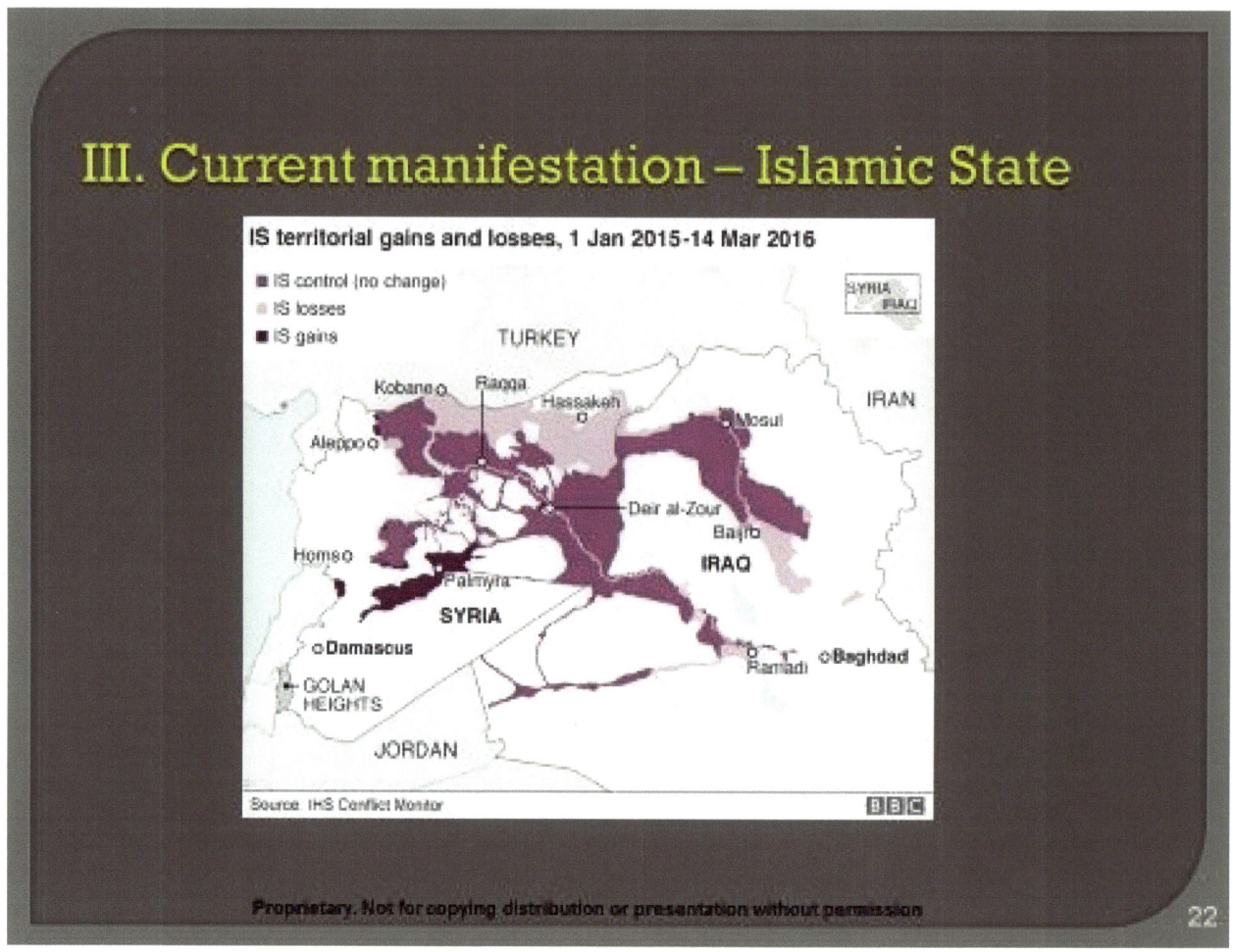

Having seen all the failures in the Arab World and the acute frustrations among the citizens of those countries, the Islamic State moved in. It offered a vision of returning to a period of greatness. This vision involved using force of arms and conquering territory, and the Islamic State occupied Eastern Syria and Western Iraq. It has been pushed back in both places, and in 2017 it may be pushed out altogether—certainly in Iraq, but maybe in Syria also.

In order to succeed, the Islamic State used ethnicity and sectarianism very effectively to sow dissent. Its orders to the field commanders are as follows:

III. Current Manifestations – Islamic State orders to field commanders

- Shiites are to be killed at once.
- Christians can live after paying the tax or jizya.
- Jews are technically like Christians, but because of the Arab – Israeli conflict, they suffer the same fate as Shiites.
- Yazidis are to be offered Islam first, and if they refused to convert, then they should be killed.

23

- Shiites are to be killed at once
- Christians can live after paying the tax (Jizya) – a form of tax
- Jews are technically like Christians, but because of the Arab-Israeli conflict, they suffer the same fate as Shiites
- Yazidis are to be offered Islam first, and if they refuse to convert, then they should be killed.

III. Current Manifestations – Islamic State Fighters

Estimates for selected nations

NORTH AMERICA		EUROPE		FORMER EASTERN BLOC	
Canada	100	Austria	100-150	Albania	90
United States	100	Belgium	440	Bosnia	330
		Denmark	100-150	Kazakhstan	250
MIDDLE EAST		France	1,200	Kosovo	100-150
Iraq	247	Germany	500-600	Kyrgyzstan	100
Jordan	1,500	Italy	80	Russia	800-1,500
Kuwait	70	Netherlands	200-250	Turkmenistan	360
Lebanon	900	Spain	50-100	Uzbekistan	500
Palestine	120	Sweden	150-180		
Saudi Arabia	1,000-2,500	Turkey	600	AFRICA	
Yemen	110	United Kingdom	500-600	Algeria	200
				Egypt	360
PACIFIC		ASIA		Libya	600
Australia	100-250	Afghanistan	50	Morocco	1,500
New Zealand	6	China	300	Sudan	100
		Pakistan	500	Tunisia	1,500-3,000

SOURCE: The International Centre for the Study of Radicalisation and Political Violence

This table estimates the number of people fighting in Syria and Iraq with the Islamic State.

What's interesting is that the top suppliers of fighters to the Islamic State in Syria and Iraq are Tunisia, Saudi Arabia, Morocco, and Jordan. All of these countries are allies of the West.

So here we are, with four top suppliers of Islamic State fighters being allies of the U.S. and Western Europe. This perpetuates the rumors in the Arab World that the West created the Islamic State and encourages it.

In 2006 there was some talk of redrawing the Middle East along religious, ethnic, and sectarian lines to make countries more homogenous. The venture was called the Middle East project. The countries titled in red would lose territory. That includes Iran, Saudi Arabia, and Turkey. Others would gain territory, such as Kurdistan and Shiite Iraq. Some of these changes are occurring on the ground as a result of conflict. Iraq already has a Kurdish Autonomous Region. The Kurds are making moves to do the same in Syria and in Turkey.

Eastern Syria is very heavily populated by Sunni Arab, and this is where the Islamic State has its roots. Western Syria is home to many of the minorities (Alawites, Druze, Shiites, Christians). The Middle East Project map calls this Greater Lebanon, which could eventually merge with Lebanon proper.

This co-location is not unique to the Arab World; such movement has and is taking place in other parts of the world.

Some co-locations took place in a peaceful fashion; for example, Czechoslovakia broke up into two parts, Scotland had an election to split from the U.K. (which will likely be repeated), Quebec has often agitated to separate from Canada, Catalonia would like to separate from Spain, and Sudan broke up into two countries, North and South Sudan, through elections.

On the other hand, people have co-located in a sometimes violently:

Yugoslavia, for example, broke up after civil war into five countries, Kashmir regularly agitates against India, Chechnya has had two wars with the Russia, and Ukraine's East and West regions are in a state of conflict.

Clearly, people like to live with their partners in sect, religion, ethnicity or tribe.

We can come to a number of conclusions on what the West should do (or not do) vis-à-vis countries in the Arab World:

- Give them space to find their own way. Interference from outside has not worked and will not likely help in the future
- Give them time. Most of these countries have not been countries for more than sixty years and no more than ten years experimenting with representative governments
- Do not have a military presence. Military presence makes a well–intentioned perpetrator become an enemy of the majority of the people
- Do not interfere in politics. China has a lot of influence in Africa, and its influence is rapidly increasing in the Middle East, all because it never interferes in politics
- Do not support the governments directly (economic, financial, military, diplomatic, or moral); support for those authoritarian governments makes people see the West as an oppressor by proxy. It doesn't help if the financial and economic contributions go into the wrong pockets

Lastly, most Arab countries do not have a thriving private-sector middle class, which is something that Western European countries have. In order to make Arab countries more stable, they need to build a private-sector middle class through soft power. This will endear the contributors to the people of these countries.

Chapter 2
Iraq: A Desert Mirage?

The model practiced to date is to help the Iraqis implement a centralized democracy along the Western model. The workable solution is a highly decentralized representative government that relies on a functioning private-sector middle class

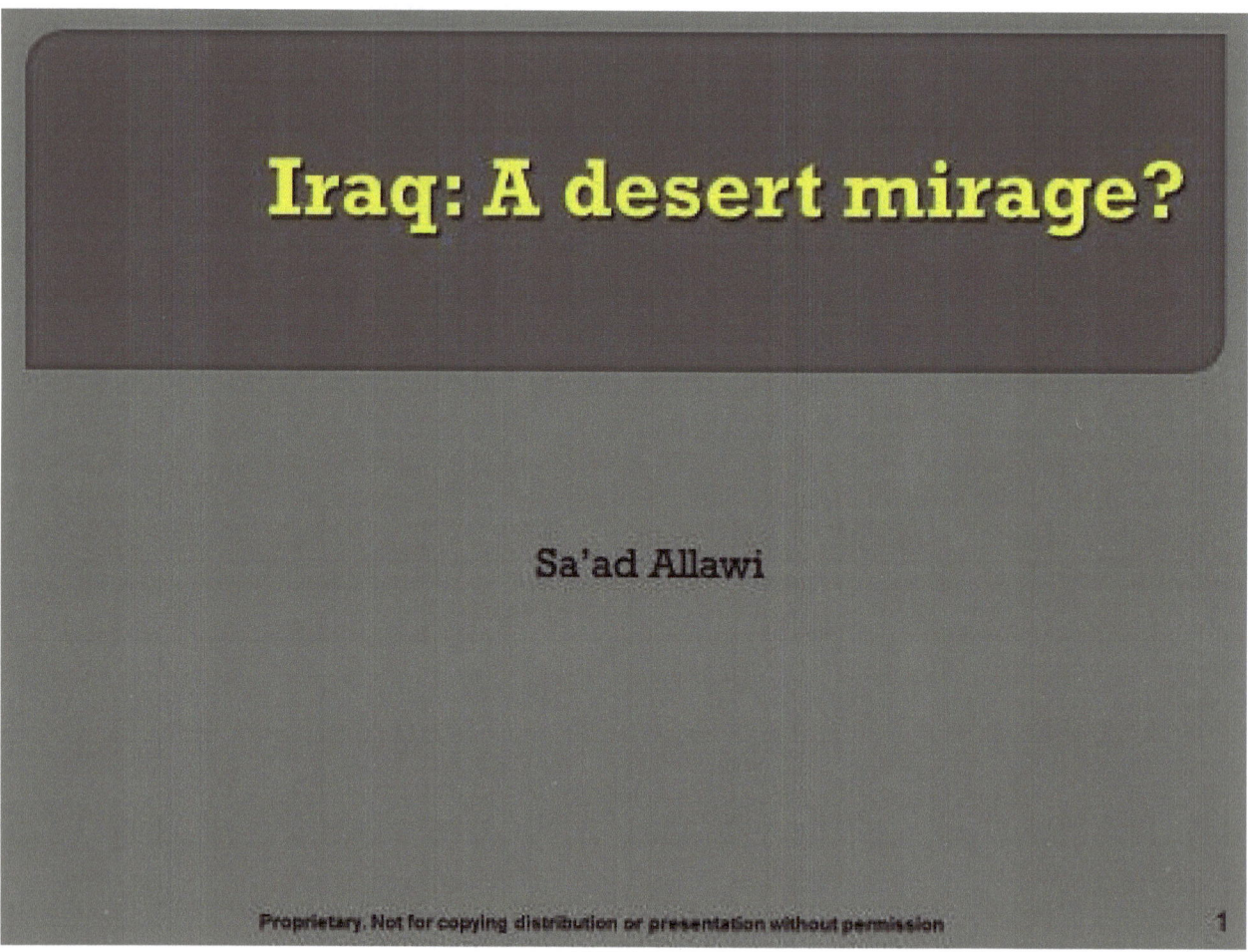

This presentation discusses the historical and demographic background of the country. It reviews the recommendations developed by the author after visiting Iraq in 2004 as an advisor to the Coalition Provisional Authority (CPA) and the effectiveness of implementing said recommendations.

It discusses the current situation/issues facing the area and the two major options for resolving them — a federal Iraq or three countries separated by ethnicity and sect.

We will cover three items

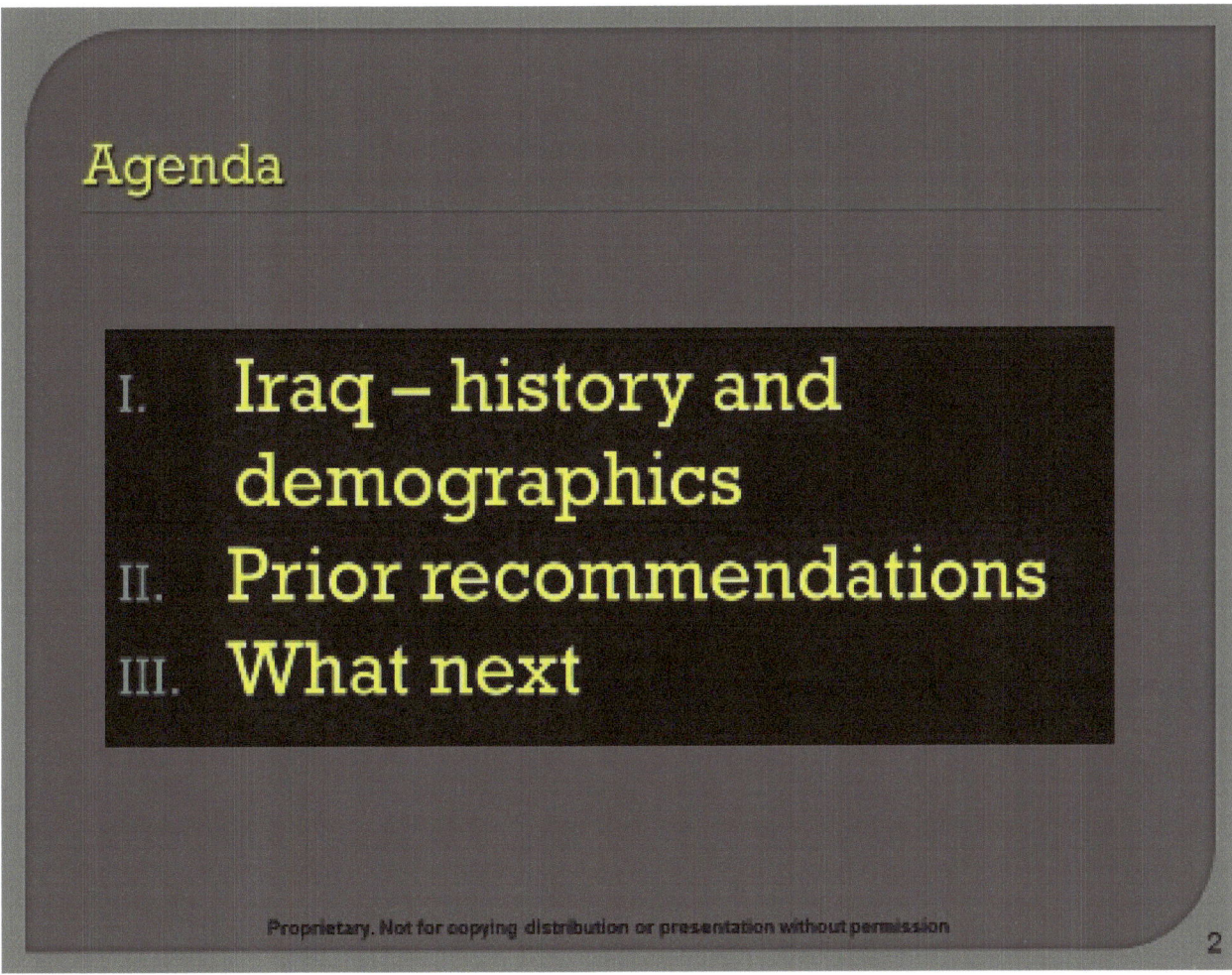

This presentation will cover the history and demographics of Iraq, prior recommendations made in 2004 as an advisor to the Coalition Provisional Authority (CPA) on the private sector development, and what is next for the country.

The map of Iraq highlights the country's demographics.

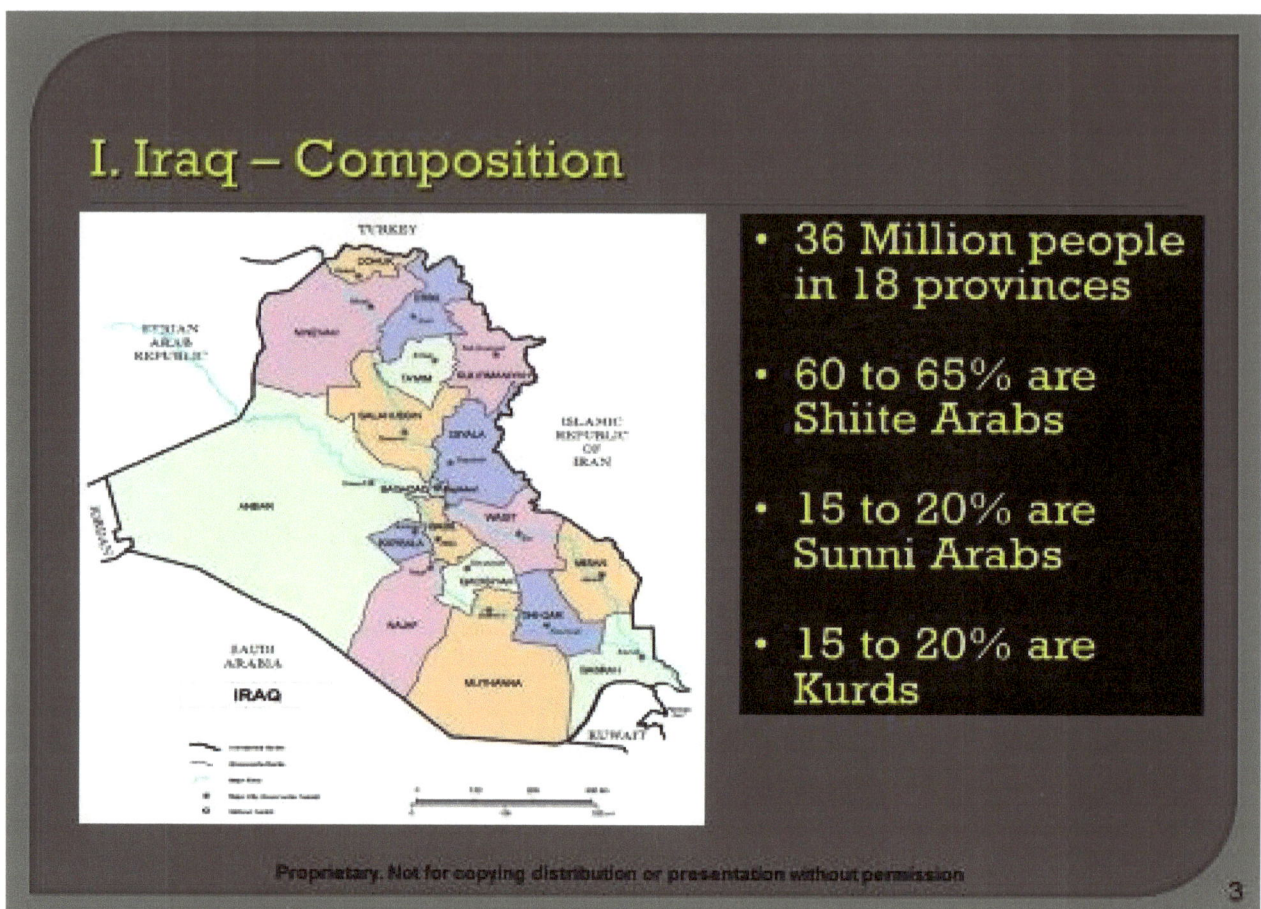

There are 36 million people in 18 provinces, 80 to 85% of whom are Arabs, and 15-20% are Kurds. Kurds are a different ethnic group from the Arabs. Kurds are Indo-European, and the Arabs are Semitic. Shiites are a majority in Iraq; they represent approximately 60-65% of the population, and 35-40% are Sunnis (both Kurds and Arabs).

Iraq is approximately the same size as California in both population and land mass.

Iraq is primarily an oil and gas country.

I. Iraq – Oil and Gas

- Proven oil reserves 143 billion barrels (5th)

- Potential oil reserves 350 billion barrels or greater (Largest)

- Iraq oil is easy to extract – ($10 -$15 per barrel)

- Gas reserves 3.2 trillion cu. M (11th)

Proprietary. Not for copying distribution or presentation without permission

4

It has proven oil reserves of 143 billion barrels, and it ranks fifth in the world for oil. The potential oil reserves in Iraq are estimated at 350 billion barrels or greater – the largest in the world. A U.S. Corps of Engineers geologist in 2003/2004 estimated that Iraq has at least 300 billion barrels of oil. A statement is often made by the major oil company executives: *"The last barrel of oil extracted from this planet will come from Iraq."*

Iraq's oil is very easy to extract. It costs between $10-$15 to extract each barrel from newer wells and between $5-$10 for the older, more established wells.

Gas reserves in Iraq are 3.2 trillion, ranking the country at 11th in the world. Until recently, Iraq had never placed great emphasis on gas. The current estimate of reserves was established after 2003, which means that Iraq's gas sales potential is even greater.

In addition to oil and gas, Iraq has several other assets:

I. Iraq – Other assets

- Holy Shiite sites (7 of 12)
- Other archeological sites (oldest civilization)
- Sulfur and Phosphates
- Two rivers (Mesopotamia)
- Arable land
- Dates

Proprietary. Not for copying distribution or presentation without permission

5

- Seven out of the 12 holy Shiite sites, which makes religious pilgrimage a major activity in Iraq
- Other archaeological sites. Iraq is the world's oldest civilization. There are many mounds from prehistoric times around Iraq which have yet to be unearthed
- Large deposits of sulfur and phosphates
- Two rivers (Tigris and Euphrates), hence the name Mesopotamia or the "land between the two rivers." It has arable land, some requiring investment in drainage to reduce the salinity
- Finally, dates. Iraq is one of the largest sources of dates in the world. In relatively recent times, there were more date palms than people in Iraq.

I. Iraq - economics

- GDP per Capita of $14,000
- Exports - $95 Billions
- Imports - $62 Billions
- 90% of the economy is dependent on oil
- Private sector accounts for only 30% of the economy
- Religious tourism

Proprietary. Not for copying distribution or presentation without permission

6

The economics of Iraq are summarized as follows: The Gross Domestic Product per capita of Iraq is $14,000, exports are $95 billion, imports are $62 billion, 90% of the economy is dependent on oil, and the private sector accounts for only 30% of the economy. Since Iraq is a major religious destination for Shiites from around the world, tourism contributes to the country's economic state.

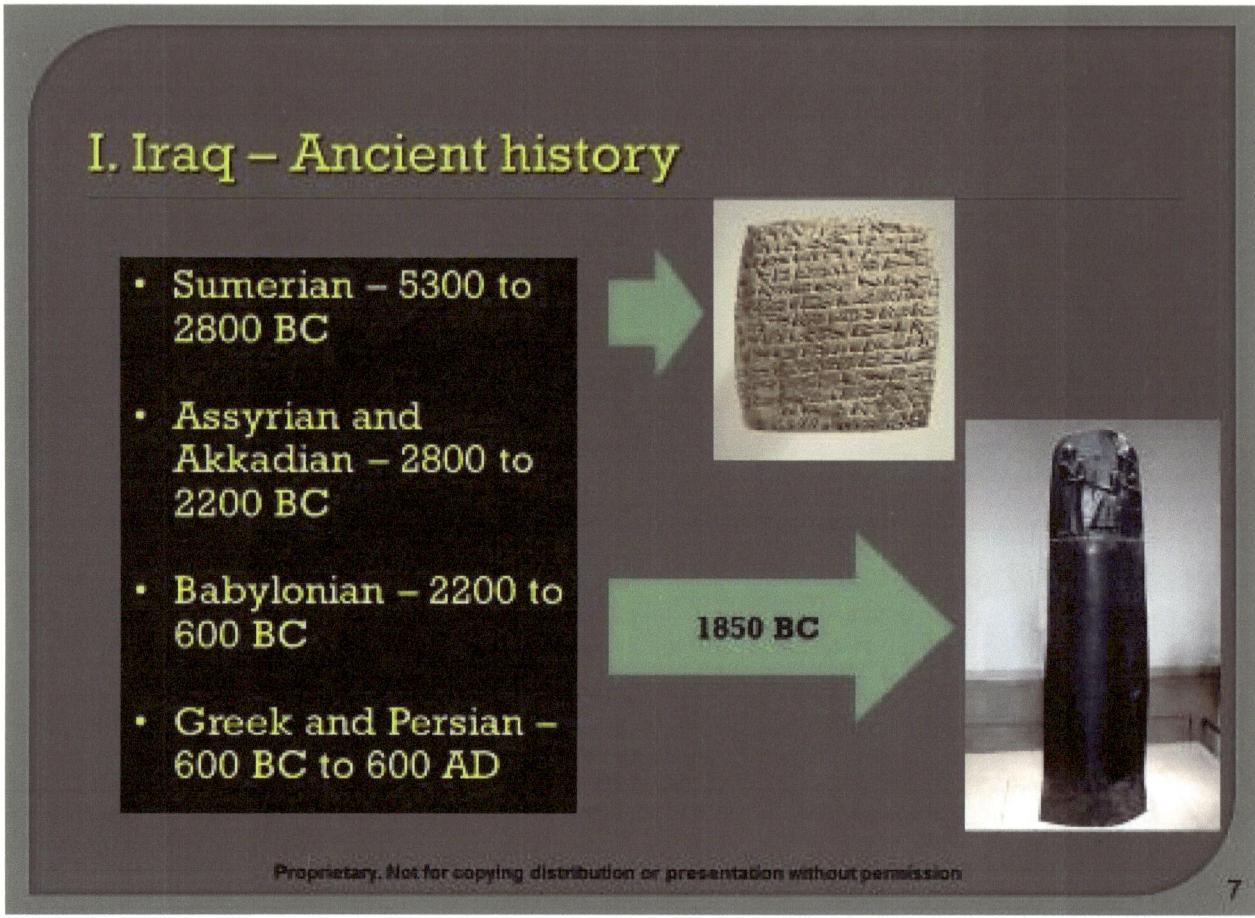

Sumerians governed Iraq between 5300 and 2800 B.C., Assyrians and Acadians from 2800 to 2200 B.C., Babylonians from 2200 to 600 B.C., and Greeks and Persians from 600 B.C. to 600 A.D.

A number of "firsts" have occurred in Iraq. Cuneiform is the oldest language in the world. It was developed by the Sumerians and is based on wedge-shaped letters. Also, in 1850 B.C., King Hammurabi of Babylonia wrote the first set of laws in the world. They are written on a big stone structure that is approximately seven feet tall and fifteen inches in diameter, composed of black volcanic rock. Half of it is commercial law, and the other half is personal law, including marital law. It resides at the Louvre Museum in Paris.

Iraq (Mesopotamia in ancient times) is the cradle of civilization.

Between 600-750 A.D., Islamic Caliphs and the Umayyad dynasty governed Iraq. Islamic Caliphs succeeded Mohammed and were based mostly in the Arabian Peninsula. The Umayyad dynasty was based in Damascus.

The Abbasids governed Iraq from 750-1258 A.D., and they were based in Baghdad. The Ottomans governed Iraq from 1258 A.D. to 1912 A.D. Then, in 762 A.D., the Abbasid Caliph Al-Mansur designed a city from scratch to become the capital of the Abbasid Empire. It was a round with four gates (north, south, east, and west), and he called it Baghdad. It was on the site of a small village, which rested on the banks of the Tigris where the Euphrates and the Tigris are closest.

Baghdad was built in 762. It was the center of the Abbasid Empire, which stretched from Spain to China.

By 1900 A.D., it was the world's largest city, with an approximate population of one million. Baghdad had a university, which still exists today, and a Wisdom Center (high powered library and "think tank"), which collected the wisdom from prior civilizations – Greek, Persian, and Roman. The city had two law schools, hospitals, a paper mill, and a coin-pressing mill.

The next largest cities were Constantinople and one or two cities in China, each of which were around 450,000-500,000 in population.

Iraq was a British protectorate between 1912-1933. The Hashemite monarchy controlled Iraq between 1933-1958. They were from the Hashemite clan in western Arabia and cousins of the Hashemite dynasty in Jordan. Iraq became a national republic between 1958-1963. The Ba'athists took control in 1963 and ruled until 2003. Iraq then became a representative republic in 2003 after the occupation.

Iraq demonstrates interesting, "bipolar" patterns as a country.

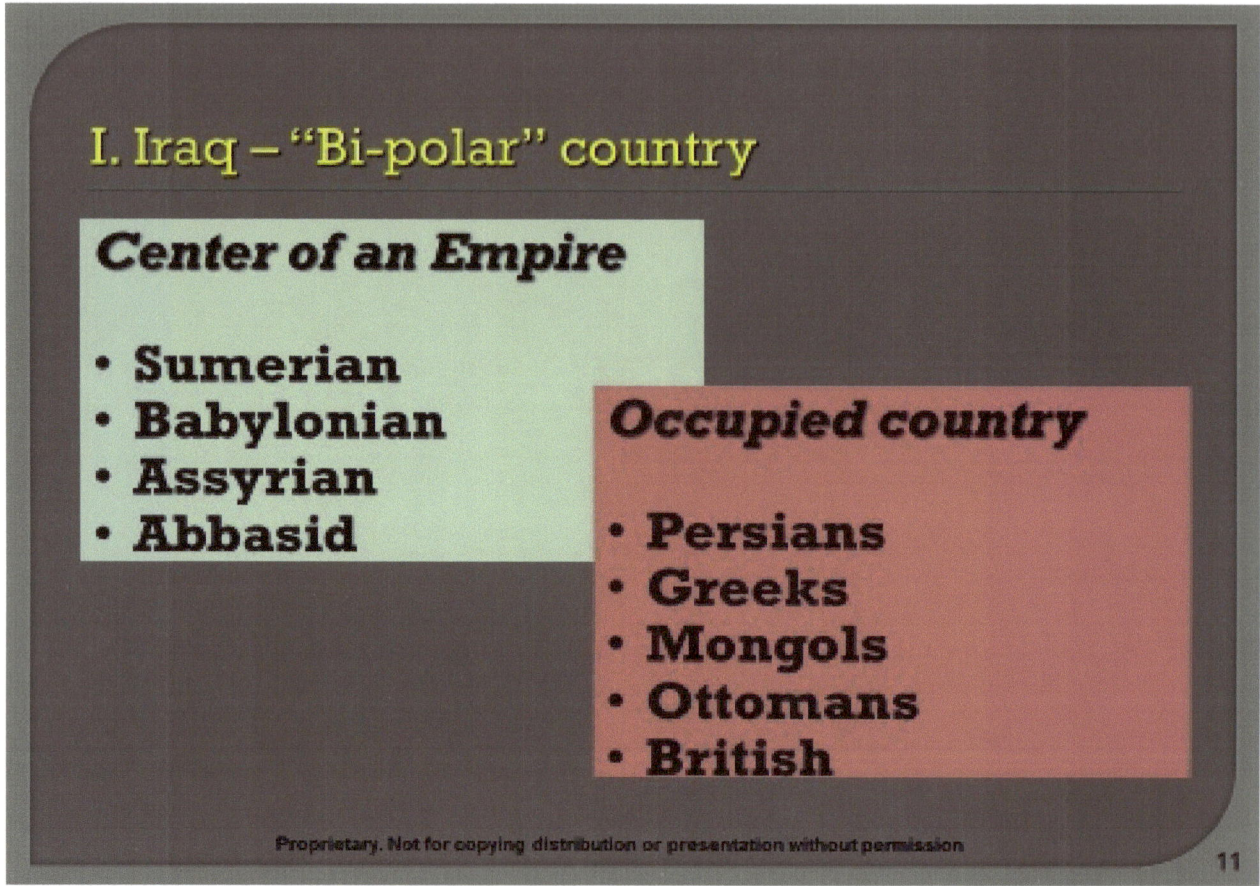

It was the center of a major empire during the Sumerian, the Babylonian, the Assyrian, and the Abbasid Empire. It was also a country under occupation by the Persians, the Greeks, the Mongols, the Ottomans, and the British.

So, unlike some of the other countries in the region, such as Turkey, Iran, Saudi Arabia, and Egypt, Iraq was never a stand-alone, cohesive country.

It was either the center of an empire or an occupied country, hence its "bipolar" history.

Iraq has seen many wars recently:

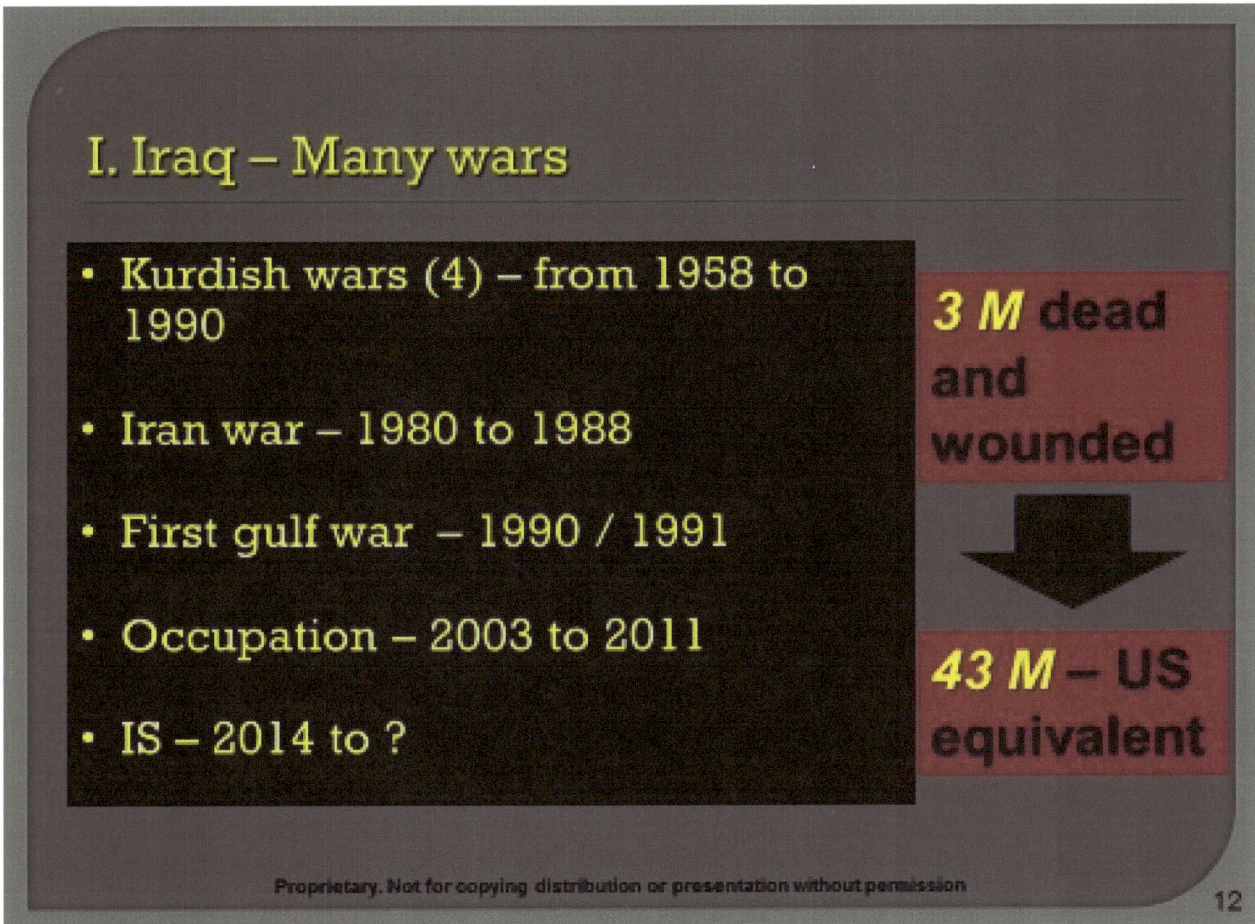

I. Iraq – Many wars

- Kurdish wars (4) – from 1958 to 1990

- Iran war – 1980 to 1988

- First gulf war – 1990 / 1991

- Occupation – 2003 to 2011

- IS – 2014 to ?

3 M dead and wounded

43 M – US equivalent

12

- Four internal wars with the Kurds from 1958 to 1990
- Iran-Iraq War from 1980 to 1988
- First Gulf War in 1990 and 1991
- U.S. occupation from 2003 to 2011
- The Islamic State occupation in 2014 to the present

As a result of all of these wars, the number of war dead and wounded in Iraq during that period beginning in 1958 is approximately three million.

Inflate that percentage to the United States based on population, it would be equivalent to 43 million people in the U.S. wounded and dead since 1958 as a result of war and strife.

The people of Iraq are war-weary.

Iraq's performance is poor. It ranks at the bottom on a global basis in a number of criteria:

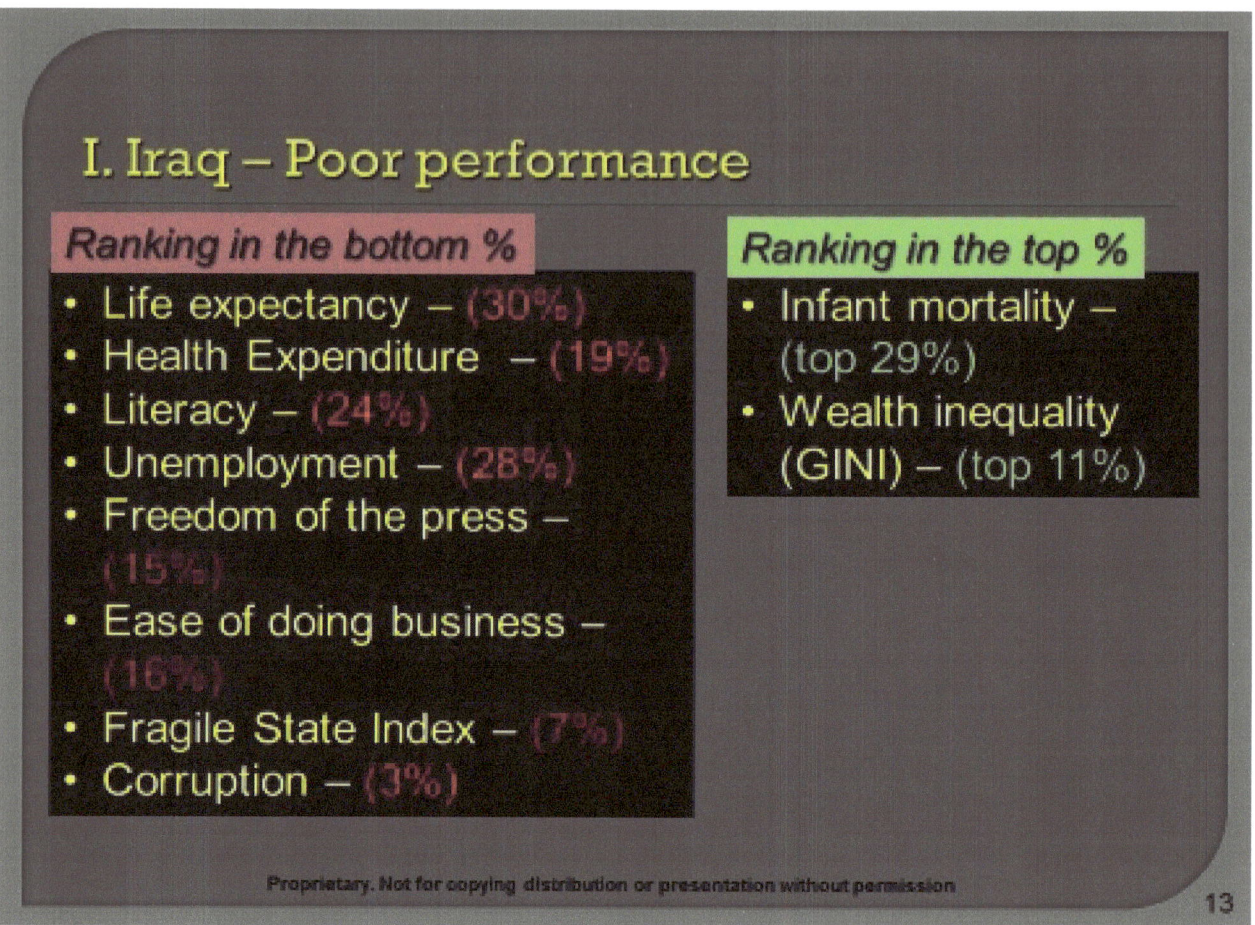

- Life expectancy – bottom 30th percentile,
- Health expenditure – bottom 19th percentile,
- Literacy – bottom 24th percentile,
- Unemployment – bottom 28th percentile,
- Freedom of the press – bottom 15th percentile,
- Ease of doing business – bottom 16th percentile,
- Fragile States Index – bottom 7th percentile,
- Corruption – bottom 3rd percentile.

There are two other rankings in which Iraq ranks a bit better: in infant mortality, Iraq ranks in the top 29th percentile, and in wealth inequality, it ranks in the top 11th percentile.

Iraq has a long way to go in improving performance.

Prior recommendations:

II. Prior recommendations – Decentralize and privatize

- Decentralize social services and private sector to the provinces

- Set national and international policy federally

- Distribute oil income to Federal programs and provinces based on population

- Develop private sector to become large part of GDP

14

In 2004, as an advisor to the coalition provisional authority, I developed a white paper after visiting Iraq delineating steps that would help make Iraq more stable and more prosperous. It had a number of key messages for the leaders of Iraq and the U.S.

First, social services (language, religion, education and health) and especially public safety (the police force) should be decentralized to the 18 provinces.

Second, national and international policy should be administered federally.

Third, oil income should be distributed to the federal programs and provinces based on population, including the possibility of writing checks to individuals just like Alaska does.

Fourth, the private sector should be developed to become a large part of the Gross Domestic Product so reliance on oil becomes less important, and it should be decentralized to the provinces.

The prior recommendations were by and large not implemented.

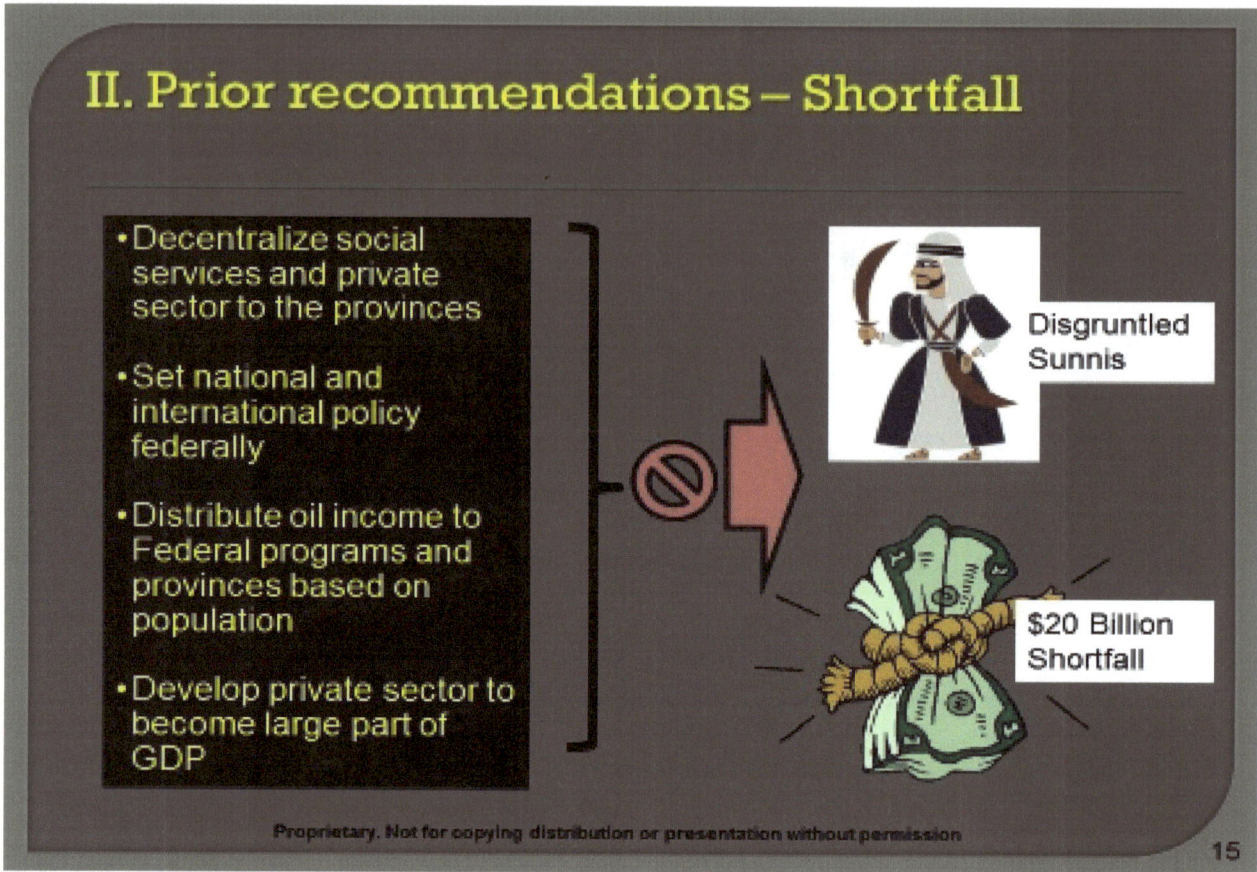

That included decentralization of social services and the private sector. Although national and international policy is being implemented federally, in accordance with the recommendations, the distribution of oil income has been an issue. The private sector has not flourished, and it's still a small part of Iraq's economy.

The end result was disgruntled Iraqi Sunni Arabs. The government ended up with a $20 billion shortfall because of the decline in oil prices.

The disgruntled Sunnis made it easier for the Islamic State to move in. The shortfall then made it harder to fight the Islamic State because there wasn't the money to do so successfully.

The Islamic State moved into the western part and the northwestern part of Iraq – left of the black line.

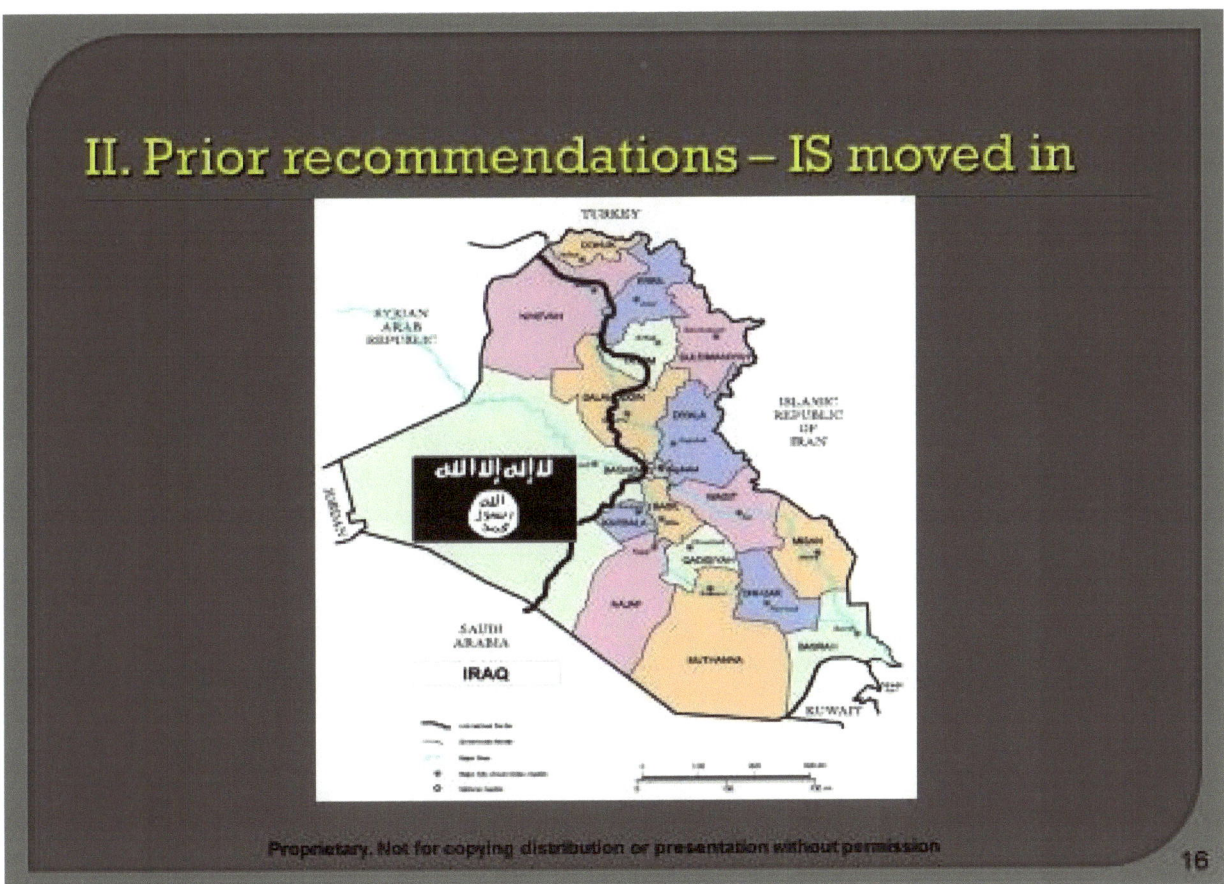

II. ISIL moved in – field commander orders

- Shiites are to be killed at once.
- Christians can live after paying the tax or jizya.
- Jews are technically like Christians, but because of the Arab – Israeli conflict, they suffer the same fate as Shiites.
- Yazidis are to be offered Islam first, and if they refused to convert, then they should be killed.

Proprietary. Not for copying distribution or presentation without permission

17

Just as a reminder from the prior chapter, when the Islamic State moved in, they used force to consolidate their power and sow dissent within the Iraqi communities. The orders to their field commander orders were as follows:

- Shiites are to be killed at once
- Christians can live after paying the tax (*jizya*) – form of taxes
- Jews are technically like Christians, but because of the Arab-Israeli conflict, they suffer the same fate as Shiites
- Yazidis are to be offered Islam first, and if they refuse to convert, then they should be killed.

Islamic State brought to the surface all the hidden ethnic, religious and sectarian tensions.

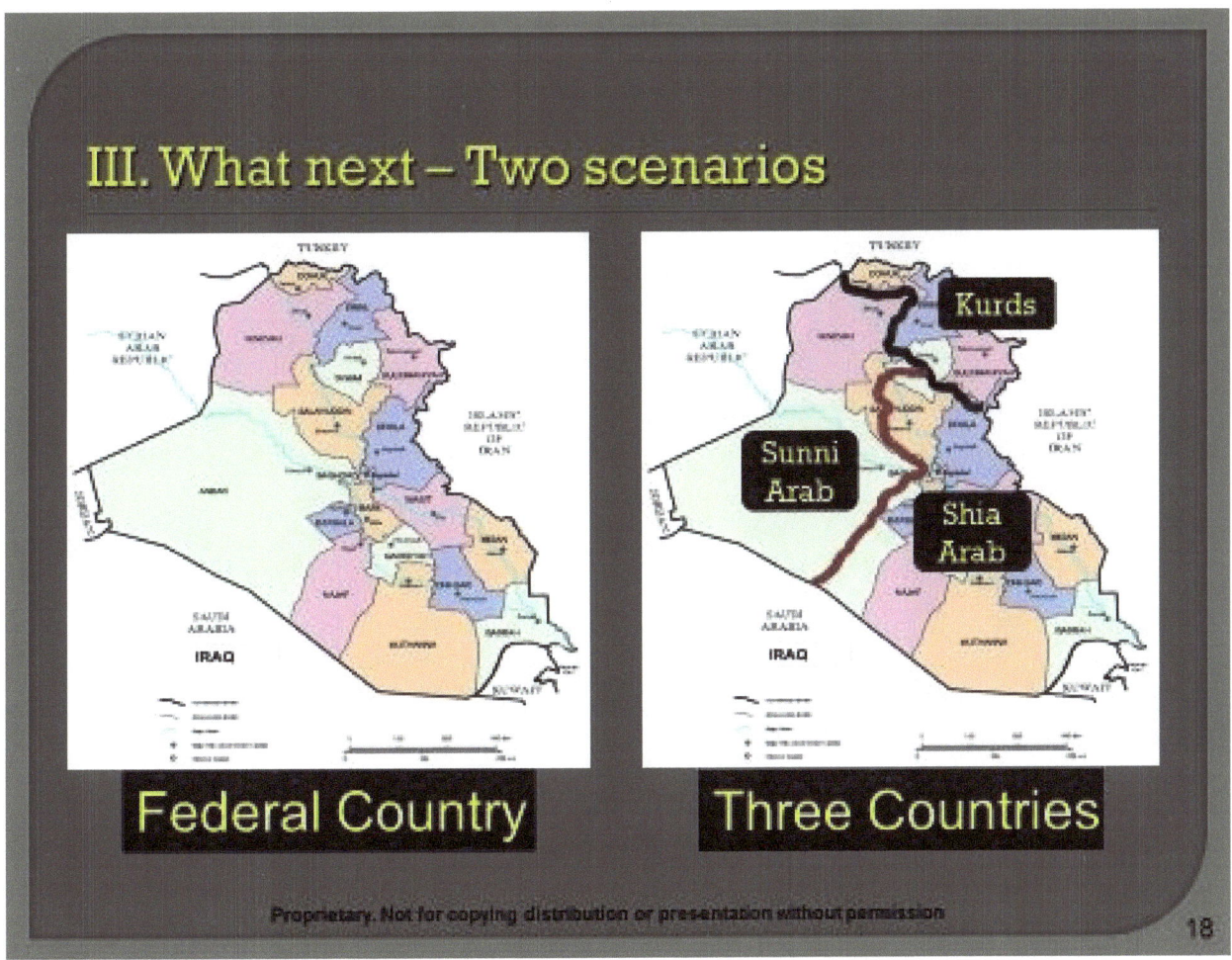

There are two possible scenarios for Iraq's future. The first is it continues as a federal country in accordance with the constitution. The second is it breaks up into three countries: Sunni Arab, Shiite Arab, and Kurd. Sunni Arab would occupy the west and the northwest part of Iraq, Shiite Arabs would occupy Baghdad and the south, and the Kurds would be in the northeast.

A federal country will face a number of challenges.

The first relates to the semi-independence of the Kurdish Regional Government (KRG) and other

Autonomous Regional Governments (ARG) that may be created. Instability will continue. The issue of segregation will escalate; where do people live who are of different sects and religions and ethnic groups?

Finally, it will depend upon the removal of the Islamic State from Iraq altogether, which appears likely at the time of the publication of this book.

Although this is a difficult option, it is marginally better than the national break-up option discussed in the next slide.

If Iraq does break up into three countries, it will face a number of key challenges:

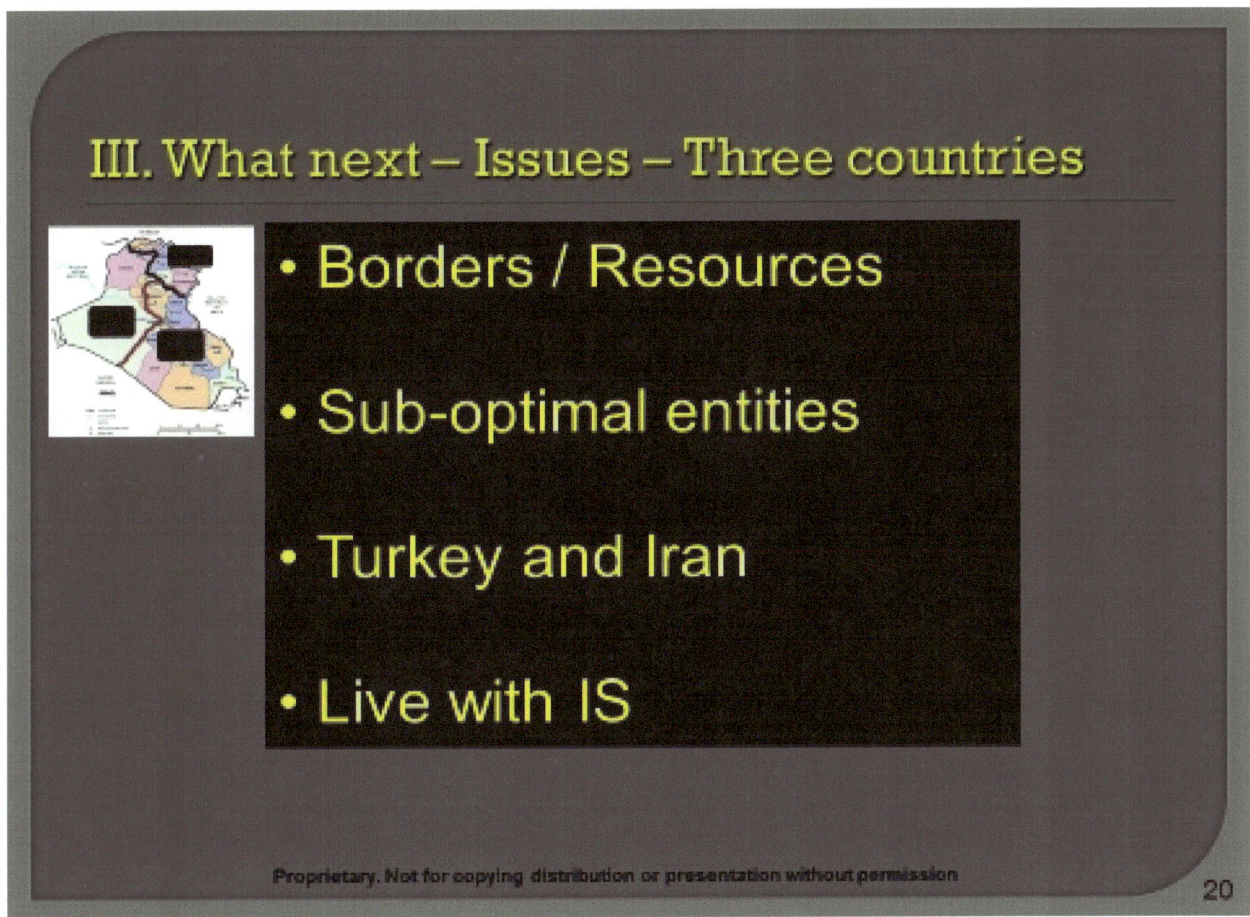

- The borders will need to be drawn in light of how the strategic resources are allocated (oil, water, and others)
- Each of the entities will become suboptimal, because they do not have enough population and resources for sustainability and some will be land-locked
- Each of these independent countries will have to deal with Turkey and Iran. Both countries will not be happy about an independent Kurdistan in Northeastern Iraq causing trouble within their own restive Kurdish and Arab minorities.
- Finally, the Islamic State (or some later manifestations thereof) will likely prevail in the Sunni part of Western Iraq.

If Iraq were to become a truly federal country, a number of changes will have to be implemented.

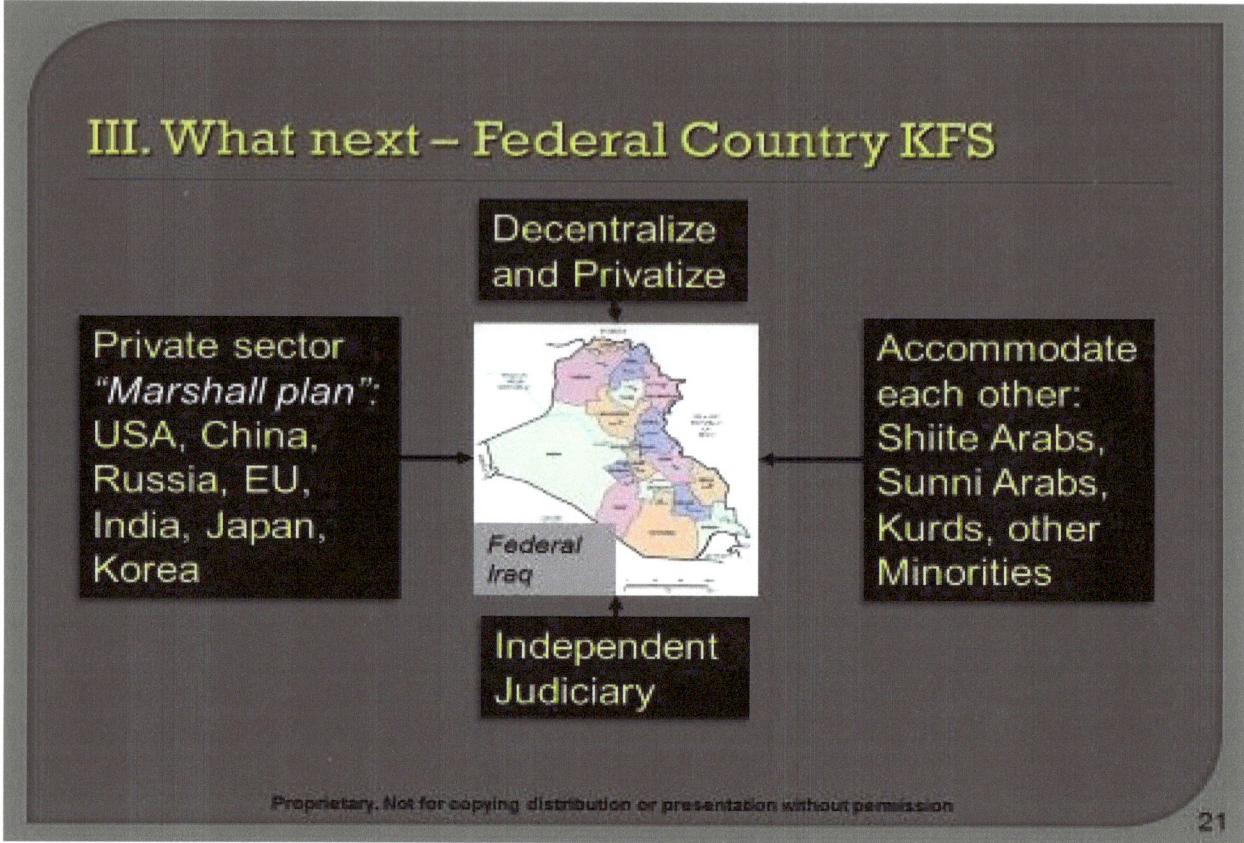

The country should be decentralized and privatized in accordance with the earlier description. Leaders will need to develop a model for the different sects and religions and ethnic groups to accommodate each other. This may be difficult initially, but it did exist for many centuries in the past. The country must then develop a truly independent judiciary. While Iraq calls for an independent judiciary in the constitution, in practice it has been under the strong influence of the executive branch. It needs to be pulled out and become truly independent. Finally, it would be necessary, for sustainable stability in Iraq, to build a thriving private-sector middle class.

These actions may require a Marshall Plan*. Major economic countries can fund the plan, including China, Russia, India, Japan, Korea, the U.S. and the E.U., to participate in building a private-sector thriving middle class. This can help bridge the gap among the amalgam of ethnic and religious groups. If successful, it could be a model for other countries with similar problems, such as Syria, Yemen, Libya, and Saudi Arabia.

*Marshall Plan - American initiative to aid Western Europe in which the United States gave over $12 billion - approximately $120 billion in current dollars - in economic support to help rebuild Western European economies after the end of World War II.

Chapter 3

Israel and Palestine: One-State Solution

The current premise is to develop a two-state solution led by the international community. The practical solution is for the two parties (Israelis and Palestinians) to create a single Federal Republic that is multi-cultural and pluralistic.

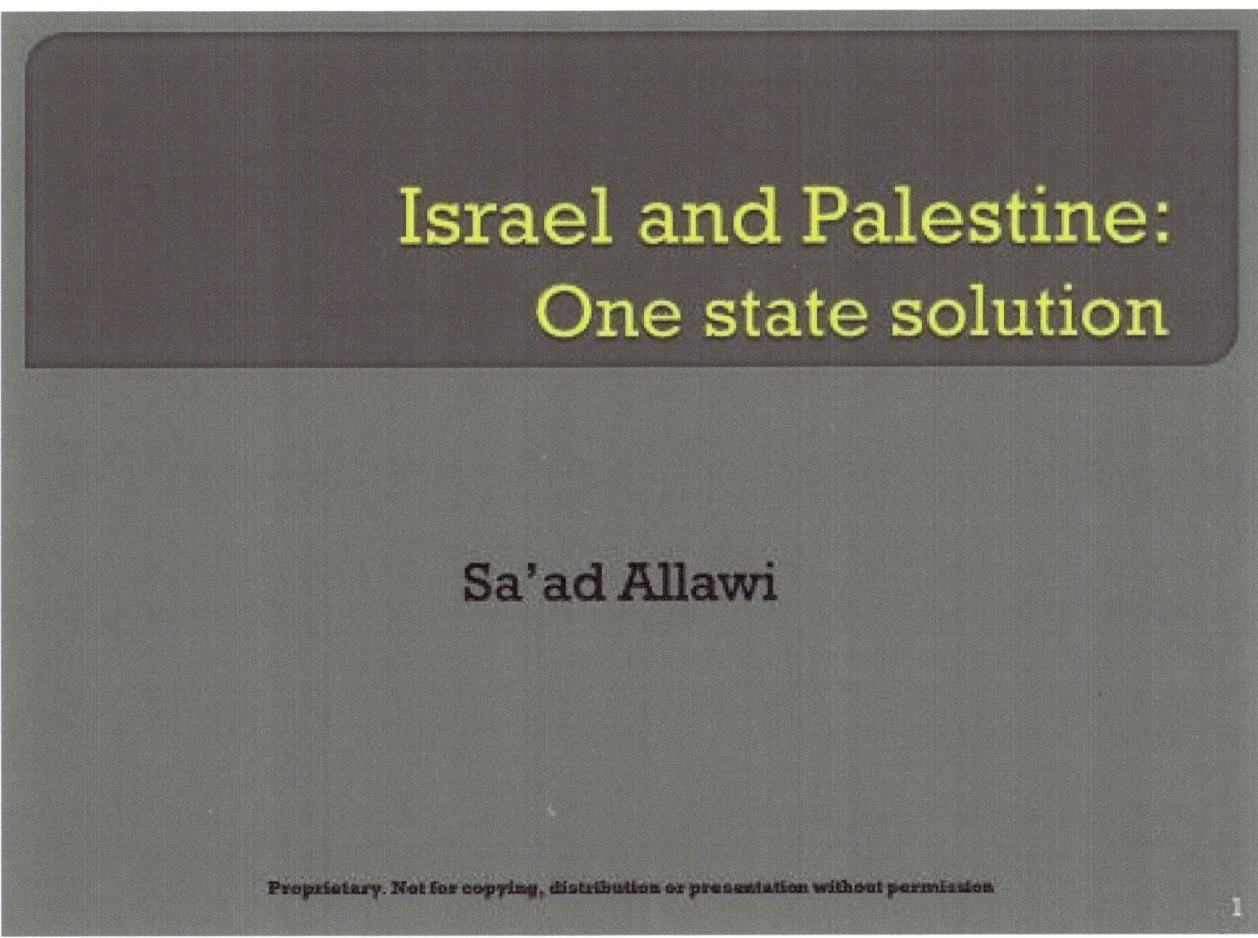

This presentation reviews the recent history, geography, and demographics of Israel and the Palestinian territories. It also discusses the two-state solution and the difficulties of implementation and provides a perspective of how a single Federal Republic State solution would be beneficial to all parties, both economically and politically.

This presentation will cover modern history, the two-state solution, and the one-state solution.

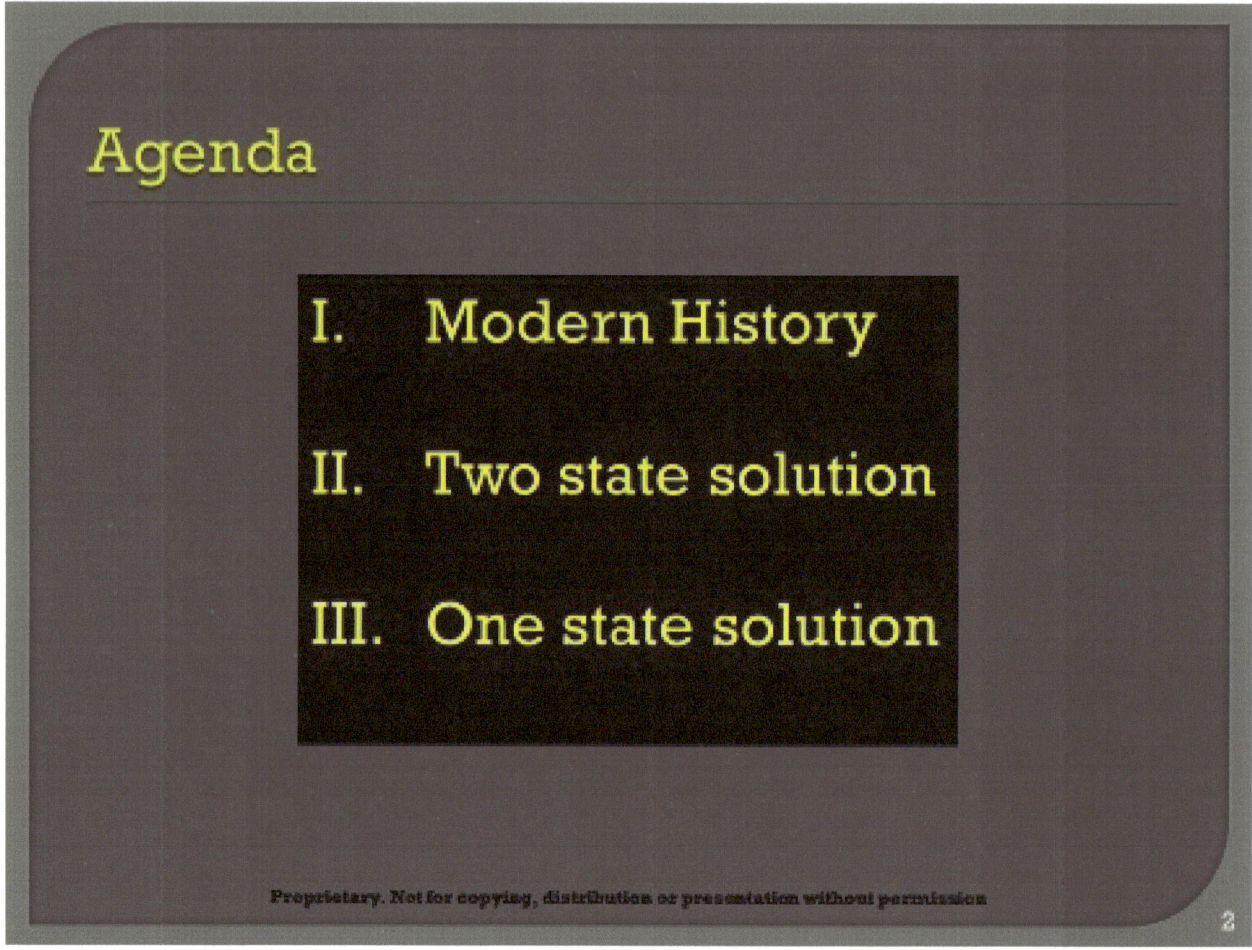

Before we start, it is important to understand that this presentation is not about:

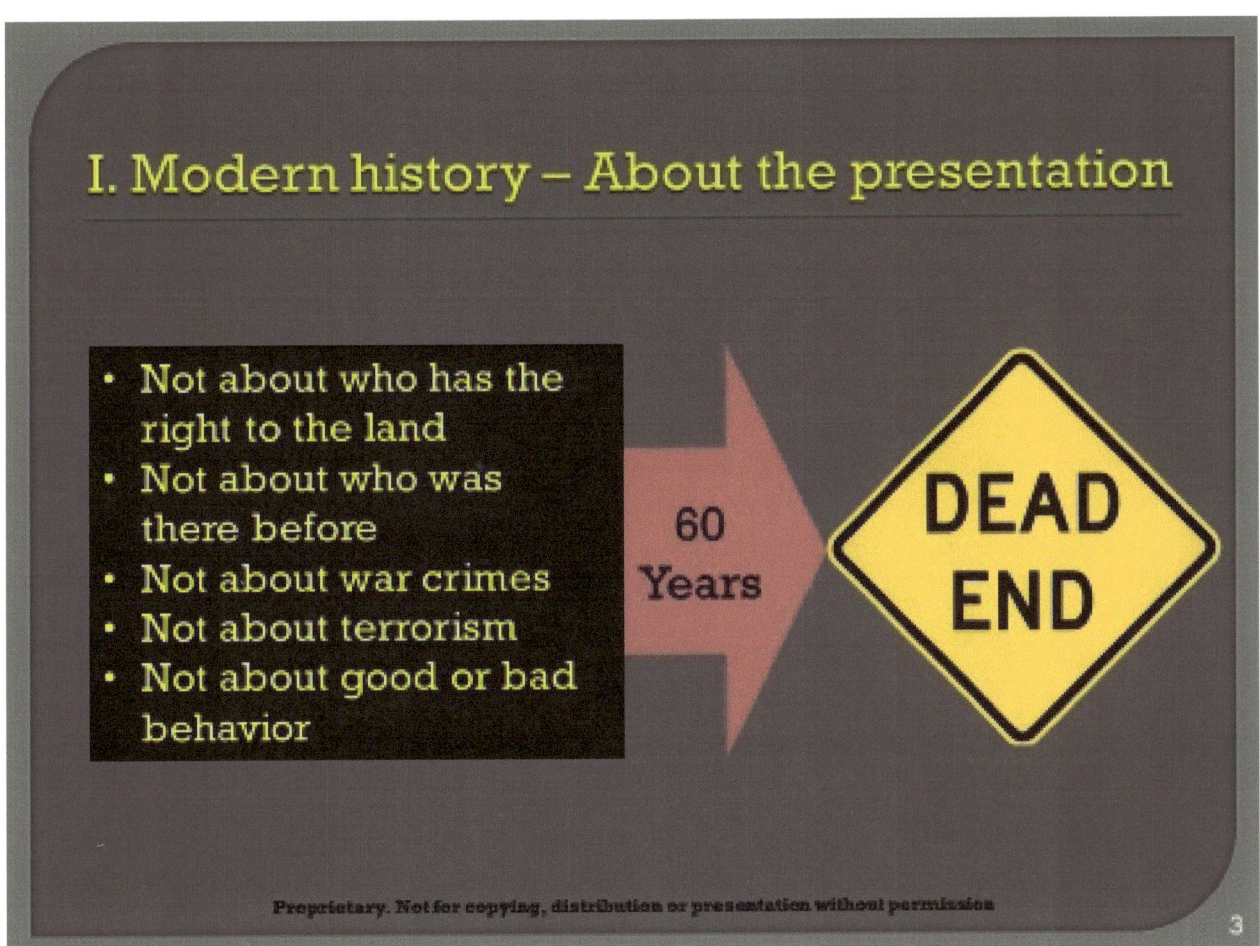

- Who has the right to the land
- Who was there before
- Who committed war crimes
- Who practiced terrorism
- Who practiced good or bad behavior

The discussions and arguments on these points have been made by both sides – the Israelis and the Palestinians – for the last sixty years and have gotten nowhere. Thus, adopting such an argument is a waste of effort and a more strategically pragmatic approach is needed

Key events in the history:

I. Modern history – Key events

- 1896 – Birth of modern Zionism
- 1917 – Balfour Declaration
- 1948 – UN creation of Israel
- 1979 – Israeli-Egyptian peace treaty
- 1987 – Founding of Hamas
- 1993 – Oslo accord
- 1994 – Israeli-Jordanian peace treaty
- 1994 – Creation of the PA
- 2005 – Withdrawal from Gaza
- 2006 – Hamas wins Palestinian elections

Proprietary. Not for copying, distribution or presentation without permission

1896 - The birth of modern Zionism

1917 - Lord Balfour of the U.K. declared the United Kingdom's favorable view of the creation of a Jewish state within Palestine (Balfour declaration)

1948 - The United Nations voted to create the State of Israel on Palestinian land

1979 - The Israeli-Egyptian peace treaty was signed

1987 – Hamas was founded

1993 - The Oslo Accord was signed between Yasser Arafat and Yitzhak Rabin

1994 - The Israeli-Jordanian peace treaty was signed

1994 - The creation of the Palestinian Authority

2005 – Israel's withdrawal from Gaza

2006 - Hamas wins the Palestinian elections by a landslide.

Over the previous period of almost 60 years, many conflicts arose in that part of the world.

Since the creation of Israel in 1948, there have been six wars between Israel and its Arab neighbors. During that same period, Israel was involved in six conflicts involving non-state actors: Hamas in the occupied territories and Hezbollah in southern Lebanon. Also during that same period, Israel was involved in putting down two intifadas by the Palestinians in the occupied territories.

Within the space of three generations, Israel has been involved in 14 wars and conflicts with its neighbors, non-state actors, and Palestinians under occupation. People in this part of the world do not forget events from generations past. The Shiite-Sunni divide has been in place for 1400 years (70 generations). Hence, this cycle is not likely to end.

One of the smartest people on the planet, Albert Einstein, provided a definition of insanity. He defined insanity as *"doing the same thing over and over and expecting a different outcome."*

Look at the map of Israel.

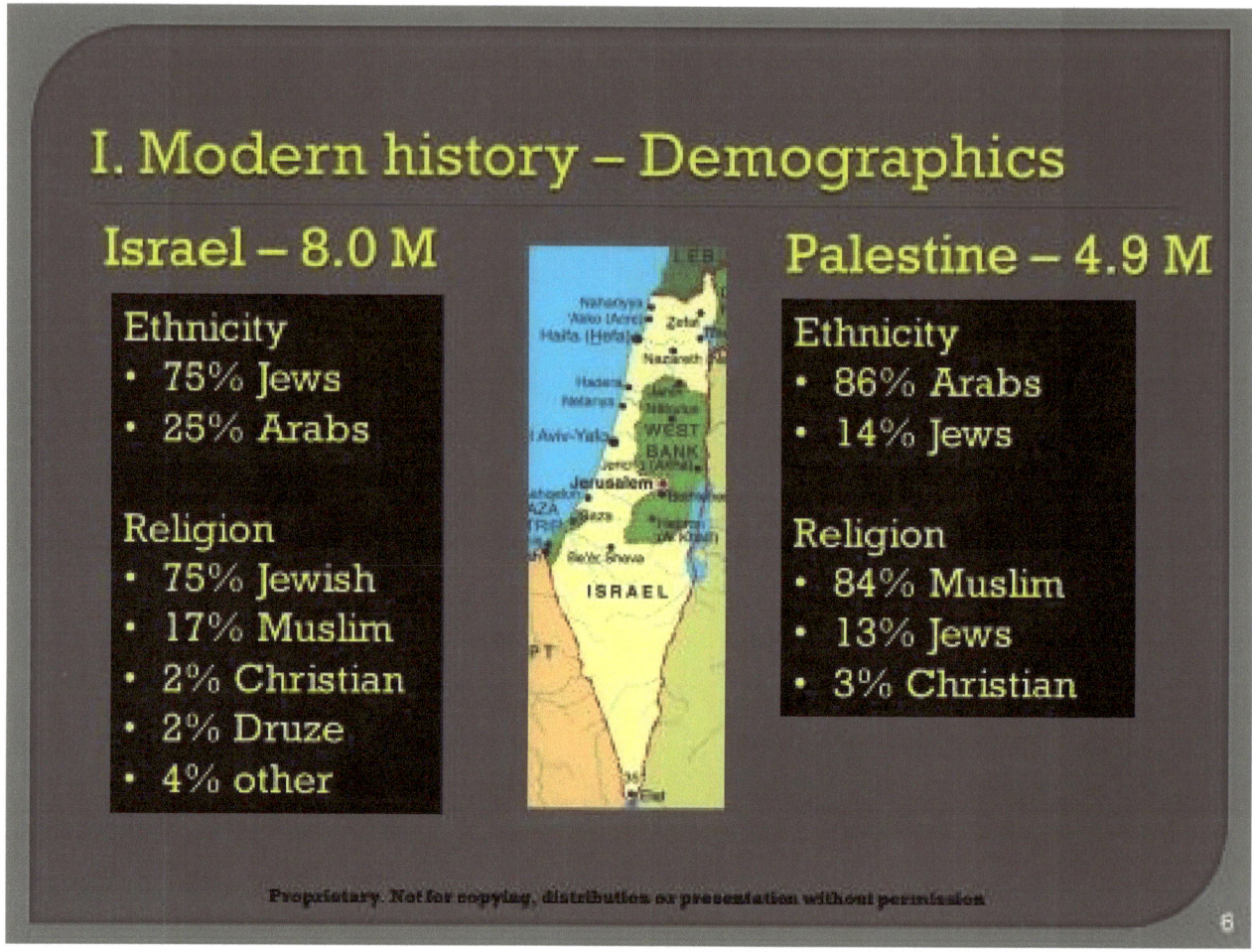

The green parts are Palestinian-occupied territories; on the left side is the Gaza strip, and to the right is the West Bank.

Israel proper (excluding the occupied territories) has a total population of eight million people. 75% of them are Jews, and 25% are Arab (Israeli citizens of Arab decent). 75% practice Judaism, 17% practice Islam, 2% practice Christianity, 2% practice the Druze faith, and 4% other.

There are 4.9 million people in the occupied territories. 86% are Arabs and 14% are Jews, 84% are Muslims, 13% are Jewish, and 3% are Christians.

This chart highlights some of the key measures for both Israel and the Palestinian Territories.

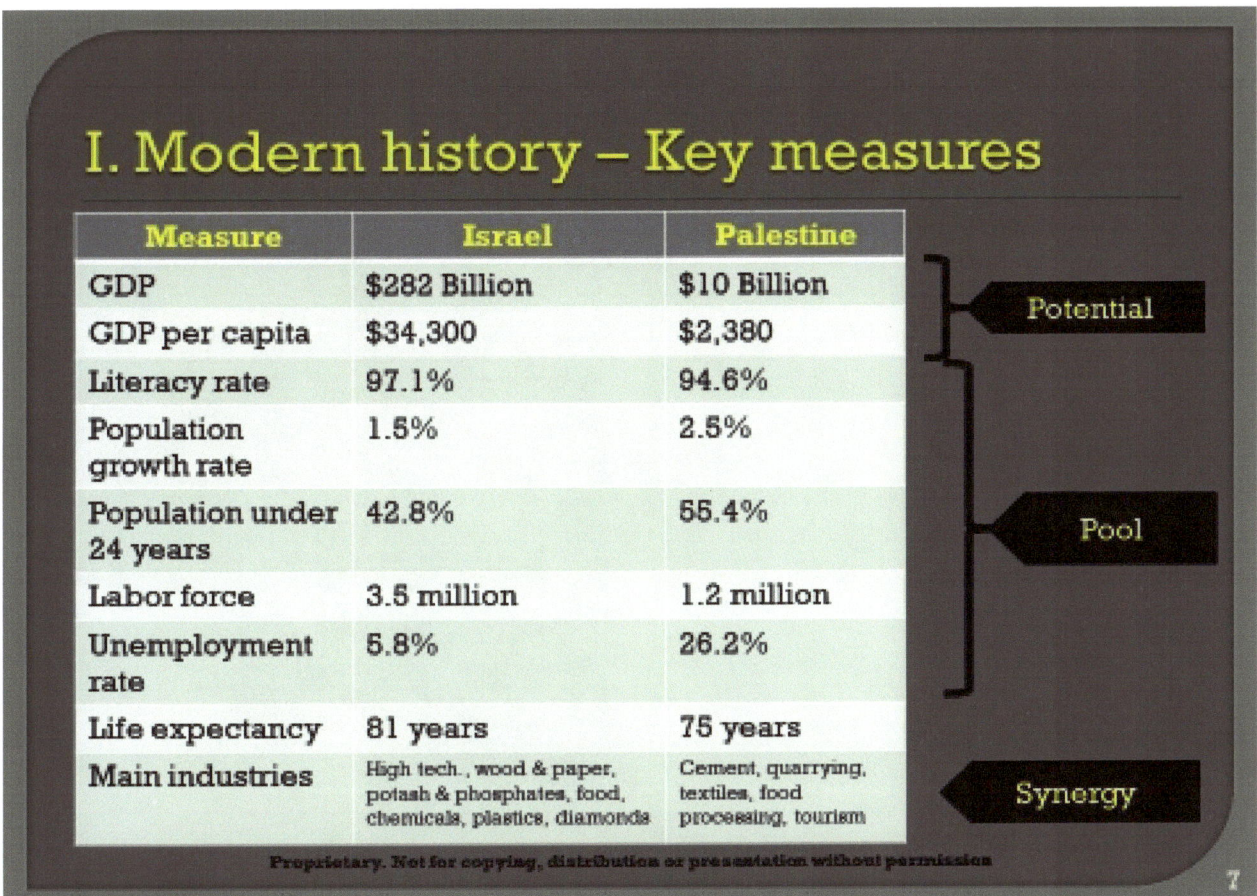

The Israeli Gross Domestic Product per capita is $34,000, while the Gross Domestic Product of the Palestinian Territories is $2,300 (Israel is about 14 times richer). The literacy rate in Israel is 97%, and in the Palestinian Territories, it is 95%. The Palestinian population growth is 2.5% vs. Israeli's 1.5% rate. The population under twenty-four years of age is 55% in the Palestinian Territories and 42.8% in Israel. Furthermore, Israel has 3.5 million of its residents in the labor force vs. 1.2 million in the Palestinian territories. The unemployment rate in the Palestinian Territories is 26% vs. 5.8% in Israel. Life expectancy is fairly similar: 81 years in Israel and 75 years in the Palestinian territories.

Israel's main industries are high tech, wood and paper, potash and phosphates, food, chemicals, plastic, and diamonds, while the main industries in the Palestinian Territories are cement, quarrying, textiles, food processing, and tourism. Examination of the per-capita Gross Domestic Product shows potential for growth. A large part of the populations is underutilized. Utilization of this population also enhances the Gross Domestic Product. There is also a large pool of human talent. Palestinians face high unemployment, while Israelis need people; Palestinians have a lot of young people, Israel needs them, and so forth.

Finally, there is a lot of synergy between the industries of Israel and the Palestinian territories. This chart is intended to show that, if joined together, there is great potential for success in both nations.

Under the two-state solution, two countries are created.

Within this map, Palestine-Israel proper is shown in tan. The Gaza Strip and the West Bank on the left and right respectively are shown in green.

Palestine will include Gaza and the West Bank, and Israel will have the remaining land. There will be corridors between Gaza and the West Bank so the Palestinians can go back and forth. Palestine will be demilitarized with Israel providing military oversight. There will be some shared resources. Discussion of the status of Jerusalem is postponed for later.

The two-state solution is difficult to implement.

II. Two state solution – Very difficult

- Very small geography – 75 m by 180 m (max)
- Movement for populations is difficult in split geography
- Status of Jerusalem is a serious impediment
- Ethnic segregation virtually impossible
  - WB cannot accommodate 1.8 m Gazans
  - Israel cannot uproot 500,000 settlers in 200+ settlements
- Population in WB intermingled
- Status of the 1.8 million Israeli Arabs
- Continued "Militarization"

Proprietary. Not for copying, distribution or presentation without permission

9

The whole country is small – 75 miles wide by 180 miles long at its maximum. The movement of population presents a challenge in a split geography, even with corridors, for both the Israelis and the Palestinians, Palestinians going east-west, Israelis going north-south.

The status of Jerusalem demonstrates a very serious impediment to any two-state solution. Ethnic and religious segregation is virtually impossible with the intermingling that is currently occurring.

If the West Bank became the Palestinian state, moving 1.8 million Gazans over to the West Bank is impossible, because the West Bank can't accommodate that many people, and the Gazans would rebel. It is virtually impossible for Israel to remove 500,000 Jewish settlers and more than 200 settlements from the West Bank. The status of the 1.8 million Israeli Arabs then becomes an issue — where do they belong? Clearly, a state of militarization will exist perpetually.

Having a single state split by a second is not a workable solution. The most recent and egregious failure in this regard was India-Pakistan.

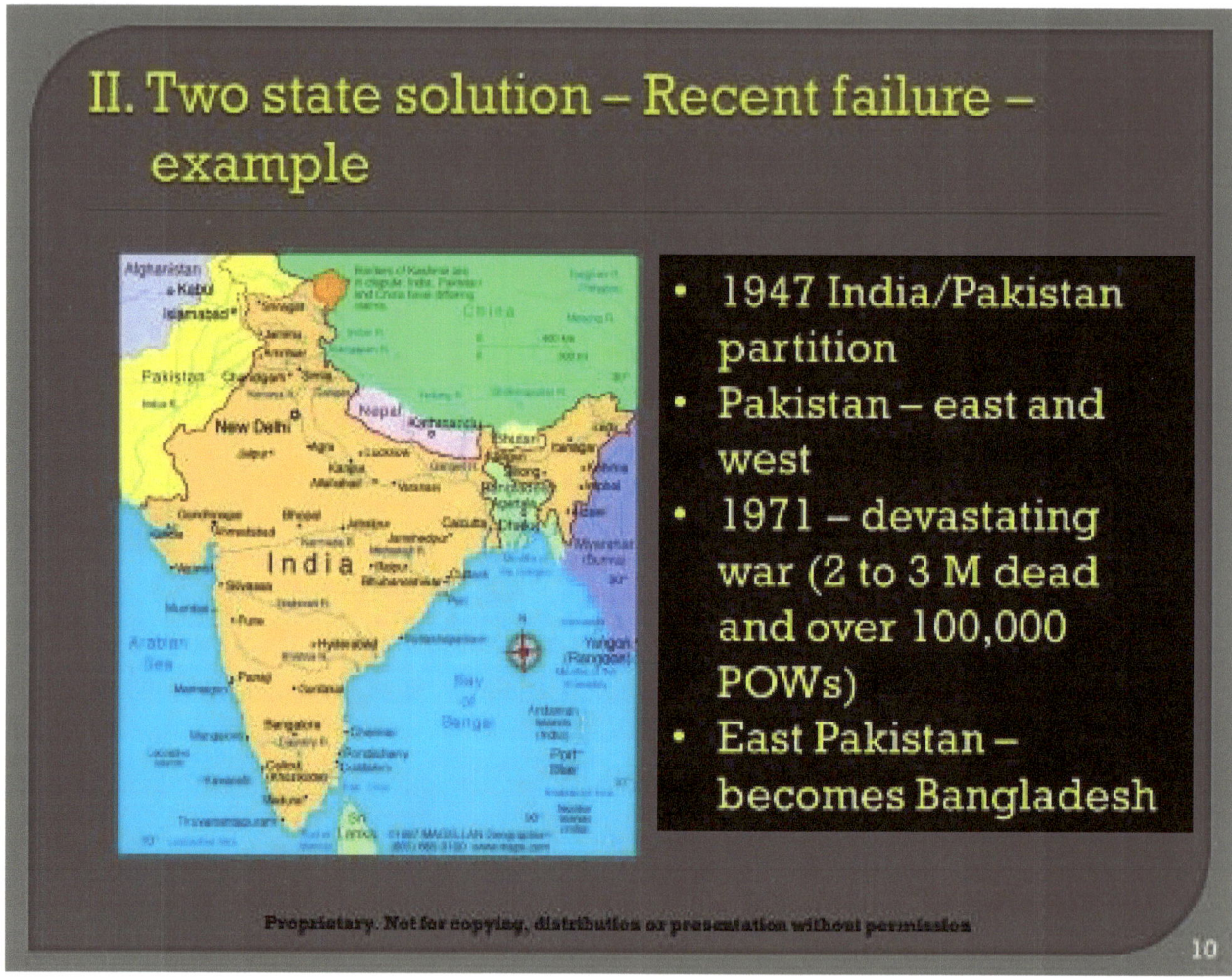

In this map, Pakistan is on the left (yellow), India is in the middle (orange), and on the right-hand side is Bangladesh (green).

In 1947, India and Pakistan were partitioned, and Pakistan became divided between East and West. The yellow part on the left was Western Pakistan, and Bangladesh was Eastern Pakistan.

In 1971, a devastating war took place. The Indians and the Bangladeshis fought the Pakistanis. Two to three million people died in that war, and more than 100,000 people became prisoners of war. East Pakistan became Bangladesh.

The creation of two parts of one country, split by a second, did not work. The same result may ensue if the Israel-Palestine two-state solution is implemented.

Listed are the highlights of the one-state solution, which resembles the Switzerland model:

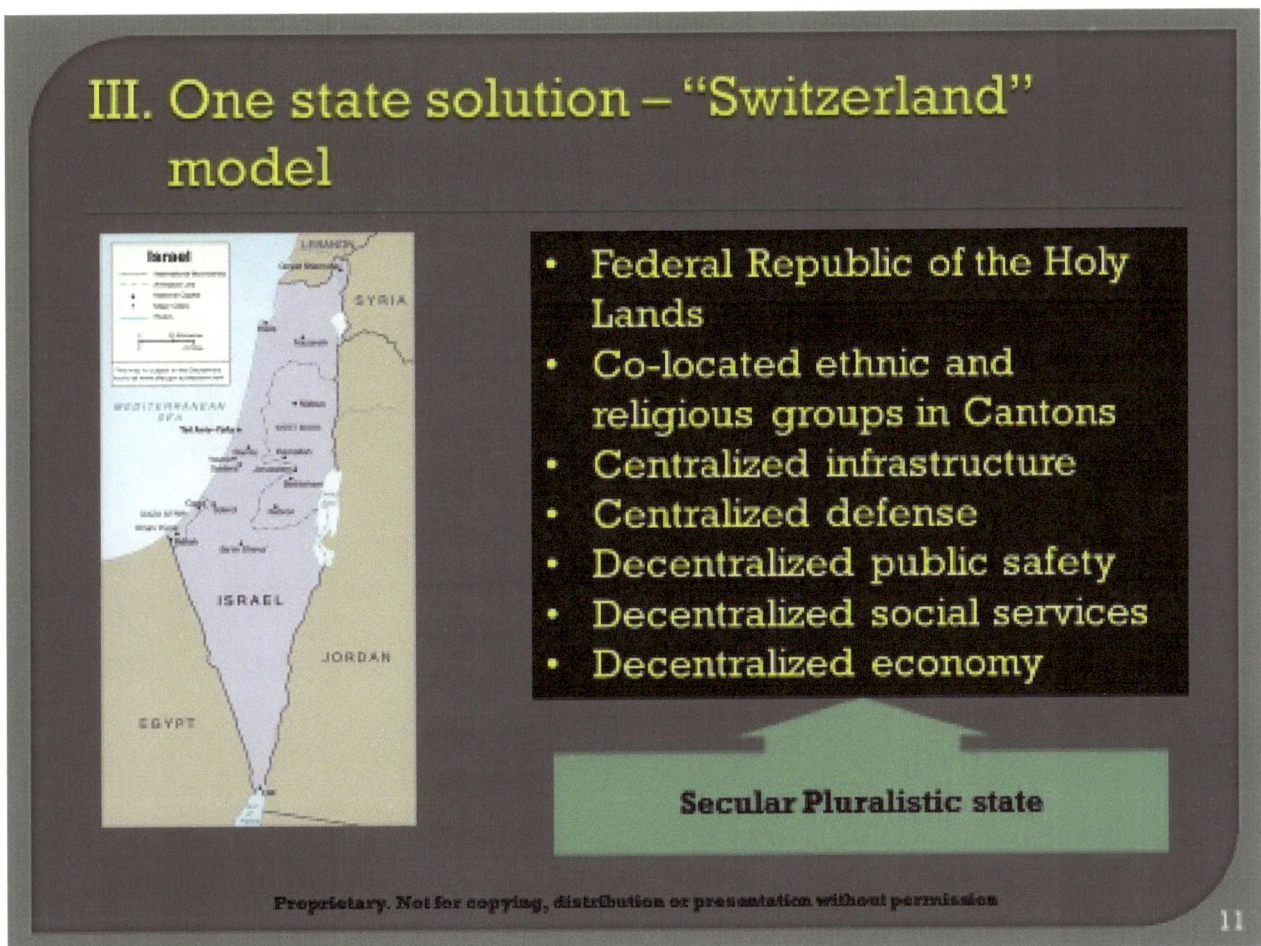

- The Federal Republic of the Holy Lands (or another name chosen)
- Collocated ethnic and religious groups existing in cantons, just like in Switzerland. Switzerland has three cantons: German, French, and Italian.
- Centralized infrastructure, centralized defense
- Decentralized public safety, i.e., the police force
- Decentralized social services and decentralized economy between the two parts
- The end product will be a secular, pluralistic state, not necessarily a Jewish state.

The potential is very good for the implementation of a one-state solution.

III. One state solution – Potential

- Synergistic industries
- High level skilled population
- Access to well educated labor force
- Lower production costs – lower prices
- Less "wealth envy"
- Jerusalem not an issue
- Shared scarce resources i.e. water and other
- Defensible borders
- Wealthy country $22,600 GDP per capita - Higher than Lebanon, Jordan, Egypt, Syria, Iraq, Turkey
- Future potential is excellent
  - Offshore natural gas
  - Religious tourism

Proprietary. Not for copying, distribution or presentation without permission

12

Such a solution involves synergistic industries and a high-level, skilled population, as seen in the chart earlier, which will offer very good Gross Domestic product growth opportunities. Such a system also offers a well-educated labor force. Palestinians (including those in the Diaspora) are the best educated group among Arab countries. Under this solution, residents will enjoy lower production costs, more labor, more production, and higher productivity. Costs will come down. Why is that relevant? Because Israel is one of the most expensive countries in the world to live in.

This solution will bring less wealth envy. When a population living on your doorstep is 14 times poorer, problems arise. This becomes less of an issue with a mingled population with greater equality. Jerusalem will not present an issue, as it will become the capital of the Republic of the Holy Land. Within this system, citizens enjoy shared scarce resources, water being one among others, a defensible border, and a wealthy country, with $22,600 Gross Domestic Product per capita – a rate higher than that of Lebanon, Jordan, Egypt, Syria, Iraq, or Turkey,

This solution will lead to offshore natural gas, and if stability is achieved, religious tourism will become a major economic activity again.

A one-state solution is a minority view currently, but it seems to be gaining traction recently.

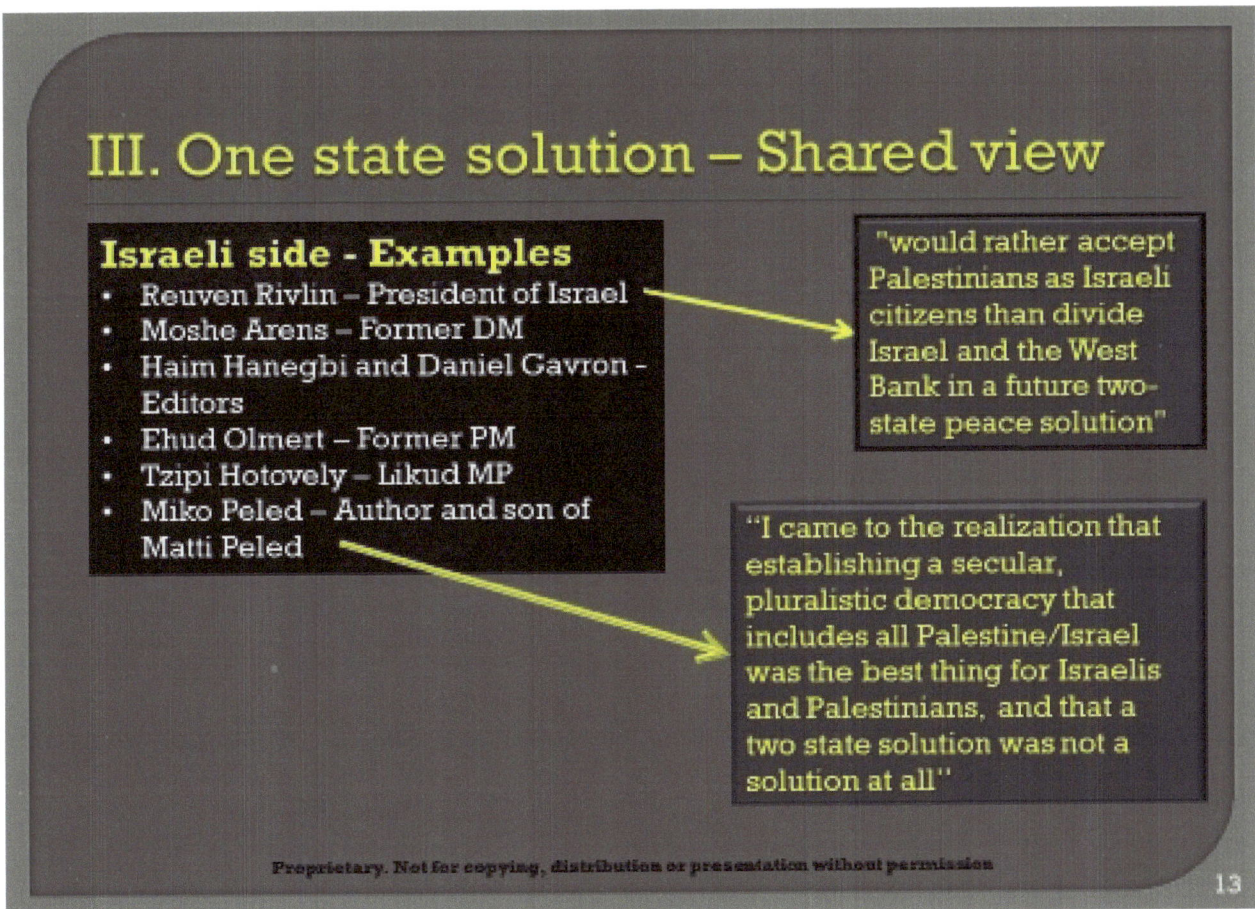

Among Israelis, some individuals who have adopted this view include Reuven Rivlin, the current president of Israel; Moshe Arens, (former defense minister); Haim Henegbi and Daniel Gavron (editors); Ehud Olmert (former prime minister); Tzipi Hotovley (Likud MP); and Miko Peled, author and son of Matti Peled, one of Israel's original founding generals.

Reuven Rivlin has been quoted as saying that he would "rather accept Palestinians as Israeli citizens than divide Israel and the West Bank in a future two-state peace solution."

Miko Peled, in his book The General's Son, said, *"I came to the realization that establishing a secular pluralistic democracy that includes all Palestine and Israel was the best thing for Israelis and Palestinians and that a two-state solution was not a solution at all."*

On the Palestinian side, the shared view on the one-state solution comes from people such as the following:

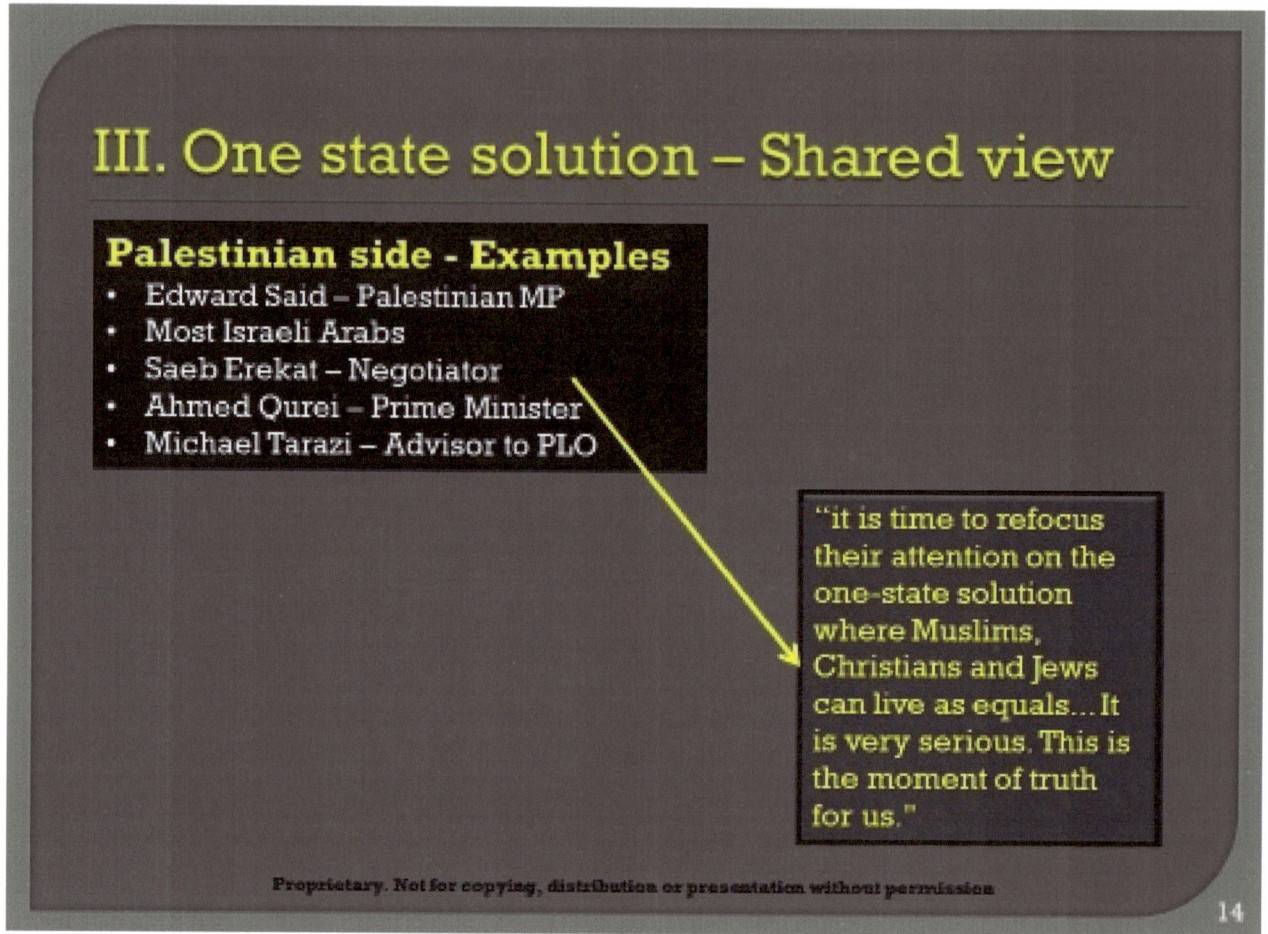

- Eduard Sa'id, a Palestinian Member of Parliament and professor at Columbia University (deceased),
- Most Israeli Arabs (1.8 million)
- Saeb Erekat, chief negotiator for the Palestinians
- Ahmed Qurei, prime minister of the Palestinian Authority
- Michael Tarazi, advisor for the PLO

Saeb Erekat said, *"It is time to refocus their attention on one-state solution where Muslims, Christians, and Jews can live as equals. It is very serious. This is the moment of truth for us on both the Palestinian side and the Israeli side to come up with a solution."*

The pressure on the Palestinian side to settle will continue and likely increase.

The industrialized nations have told Hamas that they will no longer reconstruct Gaza if another war were to erupt. Approximately one third of buildings in Gaza were destroyed in the last war (in 2014).

Mahmoud Abbas, the head of the Palestinian Authority, is aging. A younger group of people who will likely succeed him will have a different perspective on the situation, including the legitimacy of the Palestinian Authority and its direction, given that Hamas won the last free election in 2006.

Egypt's current government has reestablished the military and economic stranglehold on the Gaza Strip. Finally, the Islamists (Islamic State, Al Qaeda, and their sympathizers) are putting pressure on the more moderate Palestinians to take up arms.

There is also extensive pressure on Israel to come up with a workable deal.

The first one is the BDS Movement (Boycott, Divest, and Sanction). This is a grassroots movement that has been adopted by many organizations in 23 countries (and that number is increasing) to put pressure on Israeli companies and in turn pressure on the Israeli government.

The second is the pressure from Al Qaeda, the Islamic State, and it sympathizers in the Palestinian territories and neighboring countries (Syria, Jordan, and Egypt).

There are many Jews around the world who do not support the Zionist policy of the Israeli government. For example, Rabbis for Peace object to Zionism and object to being represented by this idea around the world.

At the end of the 2014 war in Gaza, a UNHCR set up a tribunal to assess whether Israel committed acts of war crimes against Palestinian civilians. That effort has been shelved, but it almost certainly will come back into existence if there is another war in Gaza or in the West Bank.

Finally, in 2013-2014, a poll was taken in twenty-one countries during which respondents were asked whether a country's influence on the world is mainly negative or mainly positive. The interesting thing is this chart is that Israel is fourth from the bottom – ahead of Iran, Pakistan, and North Korea – in terms of negatively influencing the world.

The map of Israel and the neighboring states shows that there are 6.7 million Jews in Israel and 6.2 million Palestinians (excluding refugees in the diaspora). There are 120 million Arabs in the immediate surrounding countries (Syria, Jordan, and Egypt). 144 million Arabs and Muslims live in the next tier of countries (Iraq, Saudi Arabia, Turkey). A very large majority (90% plus) of these Arabs and Muslims do not approve of the State of Israel and do not think it should exist.

When the US was being established, immigrants from Europe came in very large numbers and very quickly outnumbered the Native Americans. The result was the creation of a new country where the natives were sidelined.

In South Africa, by contrast, the European colonizers were outnumbered by the black Africans — both in South Africa and the countries surrounding South Africa. The end result was that South Africa became a multi-cultural and multi-ethnic democracy.

Hence, historically and demographically, Israel is much more like South Africa than it is the United States, where the natives significantly outnumbered the colonizers.

A one-state solution must be negotiated by the Palestinians and the Israelis (preferably at the grassroots level); it can't be imposed by outsiders.

The UN tried that in 1948 in this land with poor results. Similarly, externally imposed solutions in the Middle East have also demonstrated poor results.

The key factors for success for making a one state solution work are as follows:

- Emphasize the positive, as described in some of the earlier charts
- Emphasize outcomes, not the process
- Emphasize future potential, not on past failures
- Sideline the ideologues on both sides.

External pressure and support will need to be removed to ensure that both parties have the incentive to come up with a workable deal.

Failure to achieve a successful one-state solution will likely mean at least three and as many as seventy generations of conflict, which may draw the rest of the world into the disagreement.

Conclusion

Do we seek to enshrine in perpetuity in the Middle East the violence, inequality, instability and desperation that characterizes today? If that is our goal, we should continue along the path of time-tested, centralized solutions that maintain the *status quo.*

Or are we ready to do something about meaningful change other than lament its absence?

Citizens in the Middle East are dissatisfied with their governments' initiatives to solve problems and improve lives. In many cases this dissatisfaction has resulted in upheavals by and/or increasingly oppressive measures by the governments. The only constant? Instability.

Decentralizing the issues and problems to the stakeholders helps solve these problems and avoids the dreaded "we know better", approach of centralized authority or outsiders.

Developing decentralized solutions requires an organized bottom-up process of stakeholders who would rally around a set shared of values and goals. The shared values and goals will help ensure that the majority are "moving in the same direction".

This approach is longer, more painful and time consuming. However, in contrast to other solutions, the results are sustainable.

Many solutions to the world's problems defy solution because no one has the answer, or conversely, too many people proffer too many answers.

There are answers to what *appear* to be intractable problems in the Middle east. This is good news. It is the bottom-up approach to listening ---- and it has succeeded worldwide in the private sector, the realm of profits *and* government. I have devoted my working life to these solutions and can attest to that.

The question is not about whether the answers exists.

They do. It is whether leadership, in its many factions, languages, parties and families, has the willpower to allow those solutions to implement themselves.

Sources of Data

Primary Sources:
- CIA World Factbook
- Organization of Economic Cooperation and Development (OECD)
- Fund for Peace
- Infoplease
- Nobel Prize website
- Transparency International
- International Bank for Reconstruction and Development (IBRD – World Bank)
- Freedom House
- Economist Intelligence Unit
- World Resources Institute
- Reporters without Borders
- International Center for the Study of Radicalization and Political Violence
- United Nations
- Eurostat
- Globescan/PIPA
- Wall Street Journal
- Manpower Group

Partial list of books and studies
- History of the Arabs – Philip K Hitti
- A History of the Arab Peoples – Albert Hourani
- Ancient Iraq – George Roux
- The Great Caliphs – Amira K. Bennison
- The Modern History of Iraq – Phebe Marr
- Inventing Iraq – Toby Dodge
- The Crisis of Islamic Civilization – Ali A Allawi
- A Peace to End all Peace – David Fromkin
- The Israeli Solution – Caroline B. Glick
- The General's son – Miko Peled

The Author

Sa'ad Allawi has been making the American workplace more productive for 40 years. He has done so by listening and forging consensus among everyone in an organization. He gets *everyone* to, "buy in."

Mr. Allawi has done this job as the co-founder and chairman of the board of Performance Logic Inc. His experience, by a coincidence of time and place, has been primarily in health care, working for NextEra, a consulting firm; chairing the provider practice of William M. Mercer, the world's largest benefits consulting company, and; directing operations improvement practice for APM, a leader in healthcare consulting.

Outside of healthcare, Mr. Allawi, a native of Iraq and mechanical engineer (Thermodynamics and Nuclear), was the director of business development for AI industries, the largest private Kuwaiti

conglomerate. He worked for McKinsey and Co., the world's premier global management consulting firm, providing services to *Fortune 100* companies and public sector organizations. Earlier, he worked for CA Parsons, a turbine generator manufacturer, and was a section leader for MW Kellogg, petrochemical design-engineers.

Mr. Allawi served on the advisory boards several healthcare, consulting, and technology companies, and advised the Coalition Provisional Authority, or CPA, on private-sector development in Iraq. He is the author of numerous white papers and 20 articles on healthcare management entities including Healthcare Forum, Clinical Laboratories Management Review, Viewpoint (Marsh and McLennan Companies Quarterly), Business Quarterly (University of Western Ontario), Hospital Marketing and Public Relations, and Healthcare Productivity Report.

Mr. Allawi co-authored **100 Top Hospitals,** a study that has become the national benchmark for gauging hospital performance. He authored a chapter of **Redesigning Healthcare Delivery,** by Boland Healthcare, entitled "Applying Performance Engineering to Healthcare Organizations."

Mr. Allawi, past President of a Rotary chapter, received a bachelor of engineering in mechanical engineering, with a concentration in thermodynamics and nuclear, from Liverpool University. He holds an MBA from Columbia University, School of Business, with a specialty in Operations Research and International Business.

www.ingramcontent.com/pod-product-compliance
Lightning Source LLC
Chambersburg PA
CBHW041500280526
45792CB00004B/1072